BIOPHILIA:

YOU + NATURE + HOME

SALLY COULTHARD'S writing has taken her down some interesting rabbit holes. From building fires to saving bees, creating sheds to the history of craft, Sally has written over twenty books, which often explore the links between nature, home, crafts and living well. Passionate about the countryside, she also describes the joys and pitfalls of smallholding in her column *Good Life in the Country* for Country Living magazine. Recent titles include the best-selling *The Little Book of Building Fires; CRAFTED - A Compendium of Crafts New, Old & Forgotten; The Bee Bible; The Little Book of Snow;* and *STUDIO: Creative Spaces for Creative People.*

This book is for James, my nature boy

An Hachette UK Company
www.hachette.co.uk

First published in Great Britain in 2020 by
Kyle Books, an imprint of Kyle Cathie Ltd
Carmelite House
50 Victoria Embankment
London EC4Y 0DZ
www.kylebooks.co.uk

ISBN: 978 0 85783 7158

Distributed in the US by Hachette Book Group, 1290 Avenue of the Americas, 4th and 5th Floors, New York, NY 10104

Distributed in Canada by Canadian Manda Group, 664 Annette St., Toronto, Ontario, Canada M6S 2C8

Publisher **Joanna Copestick**
Editor **Isabel Gonzalez-Prendergast**
Design & Illustration **Helen Bratby**
Production **Caroline Alberti**

A Cataloguing in Publication record for this title is available from the British Library

Printed in China

10 9 8 7 6 5 4 3 2 1

BIOPHILIA:
YOU + NATURE + HOME

KYLE BOOKS

SALLY COULTHARD

DESIGN BY HELEN BRATBY

Contents

WHAT IS BIOPHILIA?

Most of us feel good in nature. If you ask people to imagine a place where they feel happy and relaxed, many describe a warm, sandy beach or woodland walk. Some might conjure up images of camping under the stars, picnicking by a stream or pottering in the garden. Others talk of feeling the sun on their back, listening to bird song or a magnificent, sweeping view. Whatever the nuances in description, we often talk about being in nature, looking at nature and interacting with nature.

That's what 'biophilia' is. It's the simple, core truth that humans need a connection with nature to be content. It's the idea that people – since the beginning of time – must feel linked to their natural environment, and the other living things in it, not only to survive but to *thrive*. It's a fundamental part of who we are.

Understand biophilia and you realize why we are drawn to the seashore, to tell stories around a campfire or gaze in admiration at the stars. Understand biophilia and you grasp just how important it is to walk in the woods, breathe clean air and stare out beyond the horizon. Understand biophilia and suddenly all those jam jars of wildflowers, stolen armfuls of driftwood and carefully tended vegetable gardens make sense – we need nature much more than nature needs us.

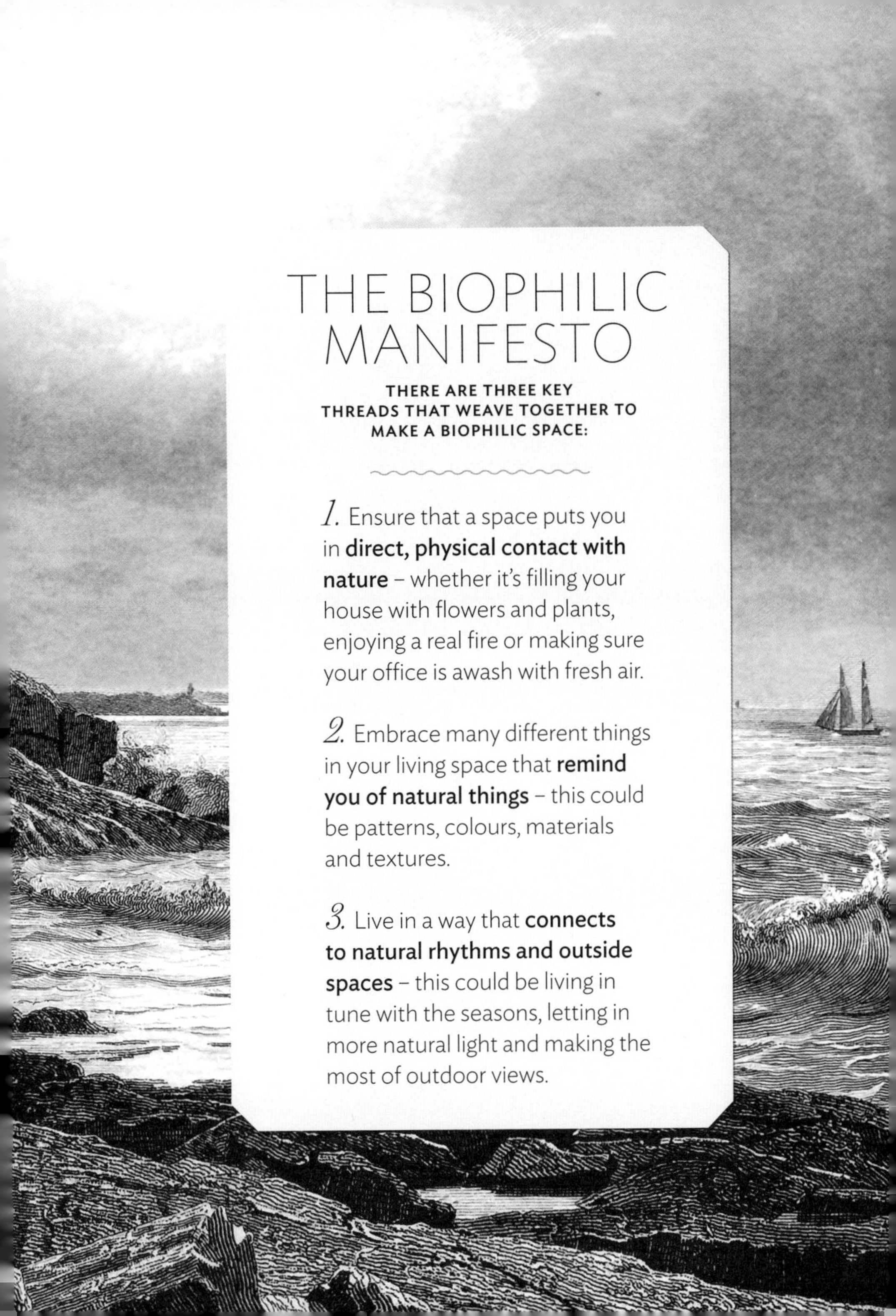

THE BIOPHILIC MANIFESTO

THERE ARE THREE KEY THREADS THAT WEAVE TOGETHER TO MAKE A BIOPHILIC SPACE:

1. Ensure that a space puts you in **direct, physical contact with nature** – whether it's filling your house with flowers and plants, enjoying a real fire or making sure your office is awash with fresh air.

2. Embrace many different things in your living space that **remind you of natural things** – this could be patterns, colours, materials and textures.

3. Live in a way that **connects to natural rhythms and outside spaces** – this could be living in tune with the seasons, letting in more natural light and making the most of outdoor views.

HOW CAN THIS BOOK HELP?

Home

It's the most significant place you spend your time in and the space over which you have most control to make changes. Use this book to not only help you think about decoration and furnishings but also lighting, indoor plants, natural light, air flow, materials, views, sounds, textures and heating. If you're planning on renovating or building your own home, you could also weave elements of biophilic design into your plans.

'Deviation from nature is deviation from happiness.'

SAMUEL JOHNSON

Work

The other space that dominates our lives is our workplace. Many of us feel that our work space doesn't make us feel inspired, happy or energized. Could you, your boss or your team implement any of the ideas in this book into your work space – such as changing your desk space, altering your lunchtime routine, or bringing plants into work? New ideas often meet initial resistance but evidence-based research into enhanced productivity, less sick days and improved morale can help the argument in your favour.

Community

If you take an active part in your community – either through school committees, village halls, rehabilitation schemes, maker spaces, community gardens, shelters, classes, youth programmes, nurseries – almost any human endeavour and social space can benefit from elements of biophilia. From bringing your dog to days at retirement homes to creating a healing gardening at your local hospital, lots of community enterprises could see tangible results from improving people's connection to nature.

HOW LONG HAVE WE KNOWN ABOUT IT?

The word 'biophilia' literally means 'love of life'. It was first used in the 1960s by a social psychologist called Erich Fromm, in his book *The Heart of Man*, and then popularized two decades later by biologist and conservationist Edward Wilson. For all their differences in approach, one theme emerged – the idea that people have an innate affinity with living things and natural surroundings. It's a concept that's been tweaked and reinterpreted ever since by disciplines as diverse as architecture, psychiatry and neuroscience.

Biophilia is also an idea that's at the heart of human living spaces. From the earliest cave paintings to classical Greek temples, from ancient figurines of the Indus Valley to the organic curves of the art nouveau, humans have always responded to nature by recreating it in their built surroundings and finding ways to celebrate it visually and with other senses. **Nature made us feel good and sustained our existence, so it made perfect sense to weave natural elements into the design of our homes and ceremonial buildings.**

That's what this book is about; how to use the principles of biophilia to help you transform your living, sleeping, working and relaxing spaces into places that inspire, invigorate and enrich your life.

WHAT COUNTS AS 'NATURAL'?

IF THE KEY TO BIOPHILIC DESIGN IS TO EMBRACE NATURE AND NATURAL ELEMENTS, IT'S IMPORTANT TO BE CLEAR ABOUT WHAT WE MEAN. THE DICTIONARY DEFINITION OF 'NATURAL' IS 'EXISTING IN OR DERIVED FROM NATURE', AS OPPOSED TO SOMETHING ARTIFICIAL OR MAN-MADE, BUT WHEN IT COMES TO LIVING AND WORK SPACES, 'NATURAL' CAN MEAN A FEW THINGS.

1. **The first is that something is literally in its purest state, as it would be found in nature;** so, an indoor plant or a collection of pebbles would be 'natural'. But most things need some kind of alteration or treatment to make them fit for purpose. 'Natural' in this sense implies a material or object that's **close to its original form** with as little processing as possible. From the 'rawest' materials – such as undyed wool or unpainted lime plaster – to more 'finished' products, such as planed timber or naturally dyed linen, the goal is to be able to **recognize and celebrate the value of the raw material**, rather than try to completely hide it.

2. **'Natural', when it comes to the built environment, is about sense of place and the idea that a building or design scheme bears some relation to its location.** Materials vary across the world – local traditions make use of natural resources to produce buildings and décor that link to their surroundings and give a space a distinct vernacular character. Design that doesn't attempt to make any connection with its surroundings doesn't feel as if it belongs to the landscape.

3. **Natural design also has to be in tune with the ways of living that are innate to humans** – a home, for example, needs spaces where you can socialize and be convivial, sleep undisturbed, feel protected and private, see what's going on outside and so on. A living space feels more natural if we can 'read' it easily and it helps us behave in a way that **supports the human experience**.

'Study nature, love nature,
stay close to nature.
It will never fail you.'

FRANK LLOYD WRIGHT

IS THERE A BIOPHILIA 'STYLE'?

Interior design trends tend to be fleeting. The great thing about biophilic design is that there is no one particular 'look'. Embracing natural elements and bringing nature into your home is a philosophy rather than a 'style' – it works whether you have an urban studio or a country cottage. Even modernist buildings, with their minimal interiors and stark spaces, can embrace some of the principles of biophilia, especially when it comes to natural light and focusing on natural finishes.

Many of the key features of current interior trends, however, do fit beautifully with the biophilic philosophy – indoor plants, micro gardens, linens, raw timber, sustainable crafts such as macramé and pottery, organic paints and warm neutrals – it seems people are instinctively discovering many of the grounding elements that come with natural design.

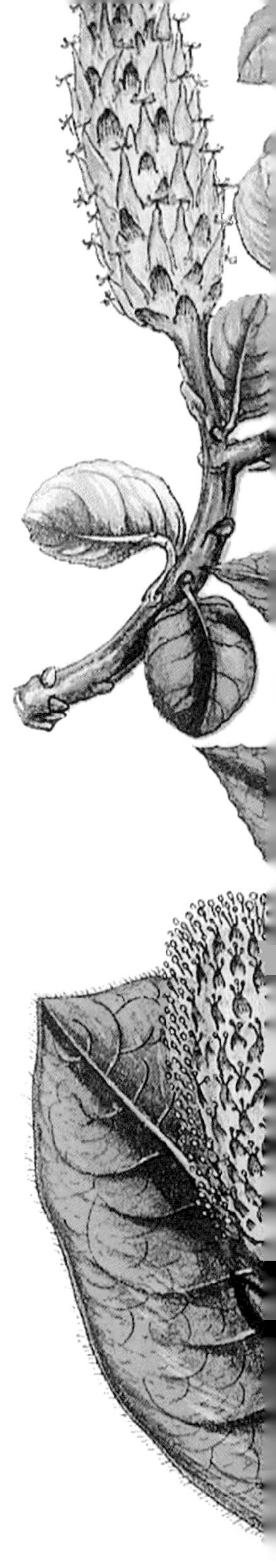

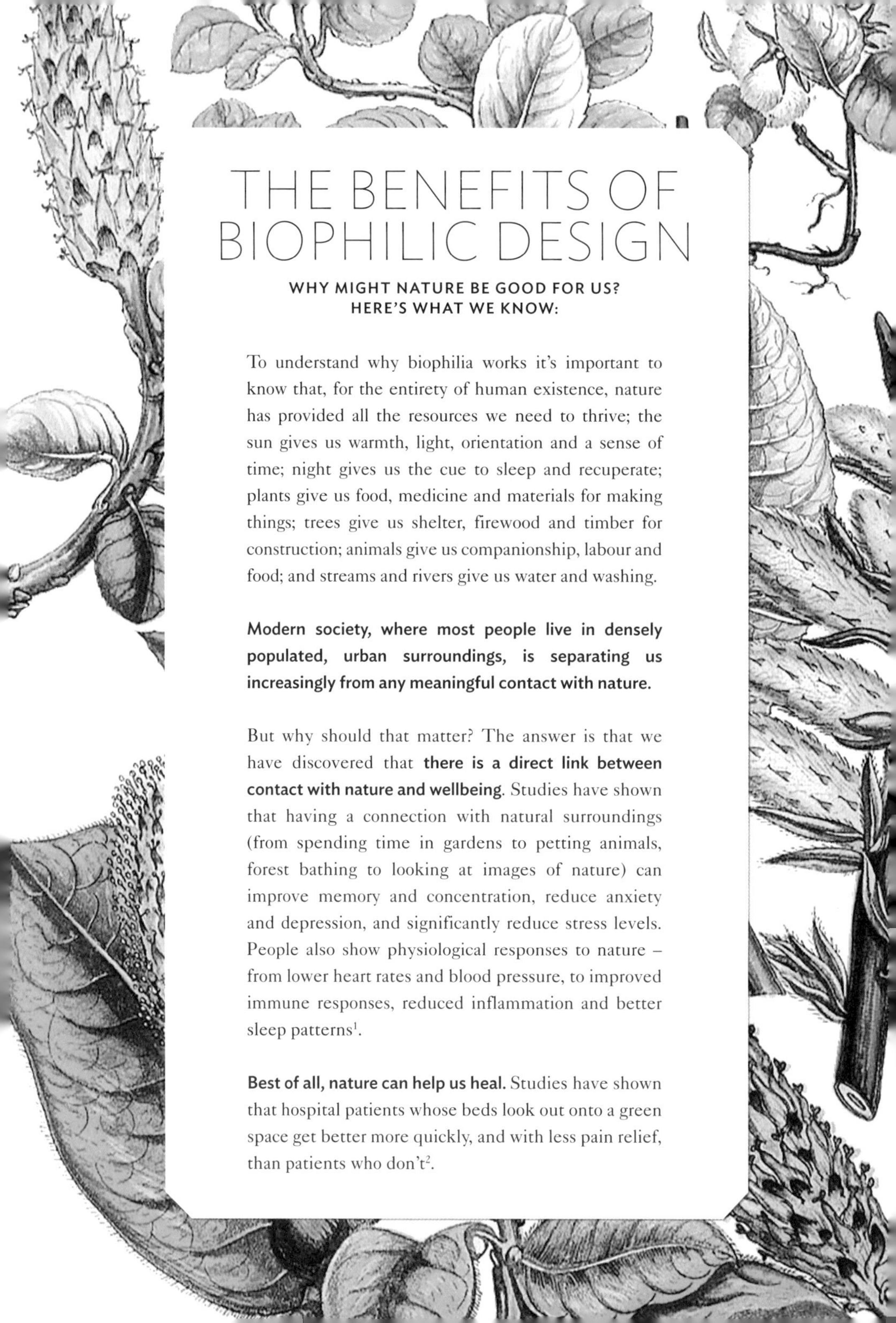

THE BENEFITS OF BIOPHILIC DESIGN

WHY MIGHT NATURE BE GOOD FOR US? HERE'S WHAT WE KNOW:

To understand why biophilia works it's important to know that, for the entirety of human existence, nature has provided all the resources we need to thrive; the sun gives us warmth, light, orientation and a sense of time; night gives us the cue to sleep and recuperate; plants give us food, medicine and materials for making things; trees give us shelter, firewood and timber for construction; animals give us companionship, labour and food; and streams and rivers give us water and washing.

Modern society, where most people live in densely populated, urban surroundings, is separating us increasingly from any meaningful contact with nature.

But why should that matter? The answer is that we have discovered that **there is a direct link between contact with nature and wellbeing**. Studies have shown that having a connection with natural surroundings (from spending time in gardens to petting animals, forest bathing to looking at images of nature) can improve memory and concentration, reduce anxiety and depression, and significantly reduce stress levels. People also show physiological responses to nature – from lower heart rates and blood pressure, to improved immune responses, reduced inflammation and better sleep patterns[1].

Best of all, nature can help us heal. Studies have shown that hospital patients whose beds look out onto a green space get better more quickly, and with less pain relief, than patients who don't[2].

Other research, from across the world, has shown that being connected to nature, either by being outdoors, looking at nature or being surrounded by natural elements can[3]:

1. Reduce cortisol levels, the stress hormone
2. Elevate white blood cell counts, crucial for immune health
3. Improve attention performance in children and adults
4. Boost focus and creativity, including problem solving and cognitive function
5. Calm the mind and boost self-esteem
6. Improve short-term memory
7. Reduce the risk of near-sightedness in children (linked to levels of daylight)
8. Encourage children and adults to develop healthy lifestyle habits
9. Increase longevity

'I shall never forget the rapture of fever patients over a bunch of bright-coloured flowers... People say the effect is only on the mind. It is no such thing. The effect is on the body, too.'

FLORENCE NIGHTINGALE

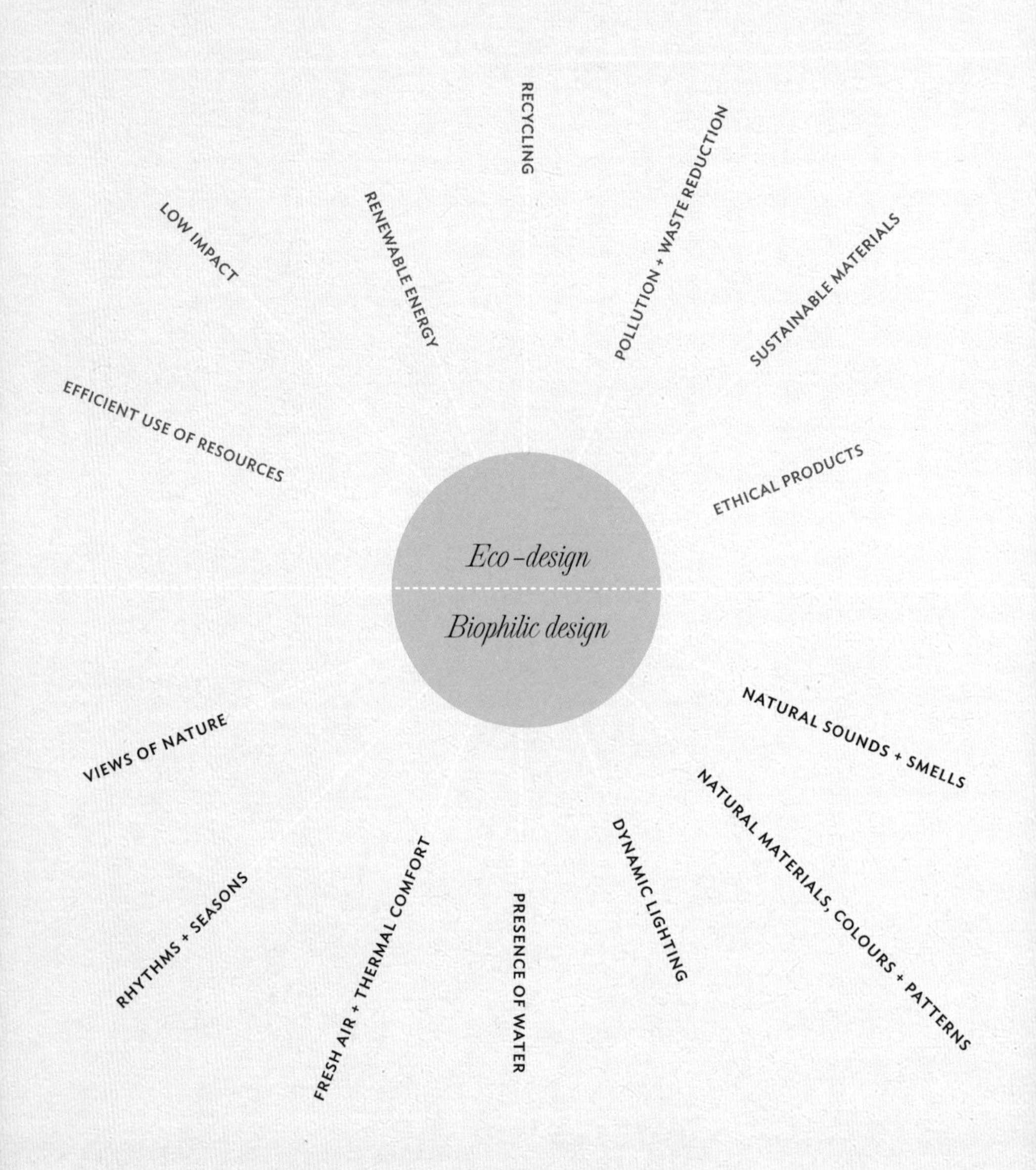
RECYCLING
POLLUTION + WASTE REDUCTION
LOW IMPACT
RENEWABLE ENERGY
SUSTAINABLE MATERIALS
EFFICIENT USE OF RESOURCES
ETHICAL PRODUCTS
Eco-design
Biophilic design
NATURAL SOUNDS + SMELLS
VIEWS OF NATURE
NATURAL MATERIALS, COLOURS + PATTERNS
DYNAMIC LIGHTING
RHYTHMS + SEASONS
FRESH AIR + THERMAL COMFORT
PRESENCE OF WATER

IS BIOPHILIA THE SAME AS GREEN ARCHITECTURE?

BIOPHILIA AND ECO-DESIGN ARE CLOSE COUSINS. BOTH SHARE THE FUNDAMENTAL IDEA THAT NATURE NEEDS TO BE TREASURED AND PROTECTED.

The eco-design movement has been around for decades, showing us how to create living spaces based on sound environmental principles and with as little cost to the planet as possible. Thanks to the green building movement, technologies such as solar energy, geothermal and recycled materials are now commonplace. The focus of green design is sustainability.

Biophilic design starts from a slightly different place – the human experience. Biophilia is essentially about improving wellbeing. By understanding the positive effect that living with nature and natural materials can bring, we hopefully make better choices about how we build our homes, institutions and work spaces, what we decorate them with, how we heat them, how much green space we have outside and so on.

The fact that biophilic design tends to produce buildings and décor that are sustainable, low impact and respectful to nature demonstrates that people's best interests and those of the environment are one and the same.

BIOPHILIA + CHILDREN

WHILE PARENTS OFTEN INSTINCTIVELY KNOW THAT KIDS GAIN A HUGE AMOUNT FROM MESSING ABOUT IN THE GREAT OUTDOORS, IT'S REASSURING TO SEE THAT RESEARCH BACKS THIS UP.

Studies have shown that nature and child development go hand in hand; play in natural environments tends to be more gender neutral, vigorous and complex than in man-made surroundings[4]; spending time outdoors decreases childhood depression and increases physical fitness[5]; and kids who develop a positive attitude towards nature go on to be more environmentally aware adults[6].

Children's spaces inside the home or school environment that include natural things (such as living plants) or mimic elements of the outdoors have been shown to boost wellbeing, mood and attention span. Other classroom measures such as increasing levels of natural light and making more opportunities for kids to see directly out onto nature also seem to increase how effectively children learn.

Ultimately, children learn about nature through immersion and being allowed to explore it in an age-appropriate way. Whether it's playing in a forest, looking after a pet or living in a home filled with plants, fresh air and natural materials, it's important for kids to have access to, and empathy with, nature.

As parents, carers and education providers, we can help children develop biophilic feelings: very young children (under sevens) learn about nature through animal stories and petting opportunities, songs and all-weather play, for example, while 7–11-year-olds love to test themselves by exploring landscapes, looking after animals, gardening and bug hunting. Older children and teenagers, often a tricky group to engage, tend to love using their knowledge of nature to build structures, learn outdoor skills such as fire-making or tracking, and get involved in social action and conservation.

*'We could never have loved the earth so well
if we had had no childhood in it.'* GEORGE ELIOT

Materials + décor

VERNACULAR BUILDINGS

For thousands of years, societies built their houses from the things they had to hand. This reliance on local, raw materials, coupled with generations of handed-down knowledge, meant that different places had distinct and recognizable architectural styles. And, because the people knew their environment inside-out, they made buildings that were designed to cope with a specific set of conditions, whether it was the weather, the geology, the climate or seasonal changes. In other words, the buildings reflected and responded to their natural environment.

Most modern buildings bear little relation to their surroundings. They use materials shipped from huge distances, standardized building techniques and styles that say very little about the culture, nature and heritage of a place. But why is this a problem?

Ecologically, many modern buildings aren't very friendly. They often have high energy costs in terms of materials, don't contribute to the local eco-system and take a lot of resources to heat, cool and light. And, because they don't take into account their natural surroundings, they often prevent the people who live in them from making any meaningful connection with their surroundings or sense of place.

It's not possible to turn back time. But what is interesting is that an increasing number of architects and designers are rediscovering vernacular traditions to create buildings that are energy-efficient and respectful of their natural surroundings. In doing so, they are also helping people live in a more biophilic way, such as using a building's natural light to its full advantage or designing in such a way as to make the most of any natural breezes that float through a space.

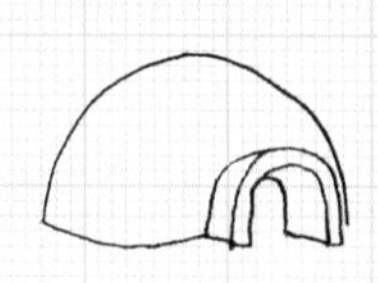

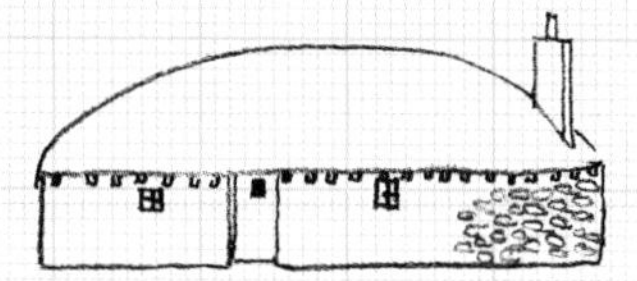

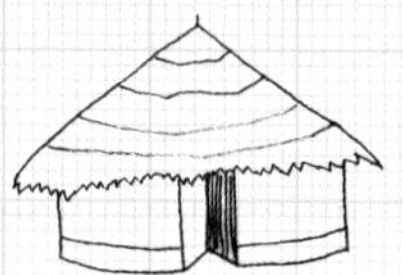

'An architect should live as little in cities as a painter. Send him to our hills, and let him study there what nature understands by a buttress, and what by a dome.' JOHN RUSKIN

With climate change as one of the greatest obstacles we will tackle over the forthcoming years, the idea of vernacular materials and buildings has never been more salient. The 'new vernacular' will need to incorporate local materials and skills with cutting-edge technology and engineering, as was the case with one recent project in Morocco. The architects behind the Technology School of Guelmim found a way to blend new, earthquake-resistant materials with ancient building traditions that influenced ventilation, air flow and the control of light. By using large north-facing windows and small south-facing ones, for example, the designers reduced the amount of direct sunlight blasting into the school, while making sure each classroom got plenty of natural light (see pages 83–87). The arrangement of the buildings also maximized the circulation of air through the space, creating a completely natural, eco-friendly cooling system.

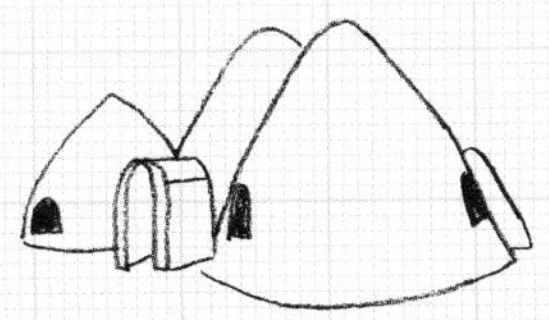
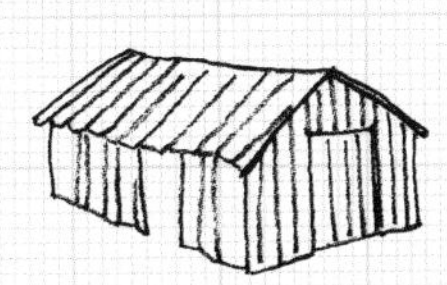
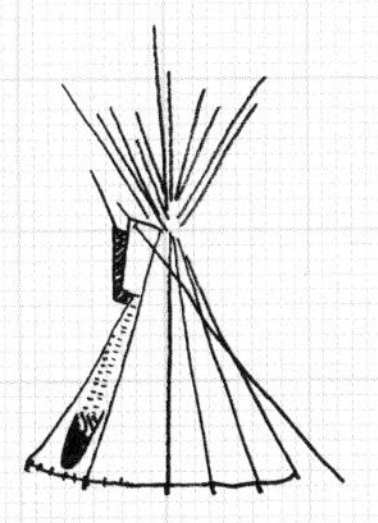

NATURAL MATERIALS

Part of this biophilic approach to materials is to use things that are as minimally processed as possible, come from your immediate surroundings and create a strong sense of place. Raw, natural materials are particularly important in this process.

On a sustainable level, using materials that have a low carbon footprint or don't use toxic processes has to be good for the natural environment. On a biophilic level, humans seem to respond in a different way to materials that are close to their natural state than materials that are highly artificial. **Living spaces that incorporate lots of natural materials give us a direct connection to the outside** – whether it's the touchable texture of a scrubbed pine table-top or the soft, luxurious feel of a lamb's wool blanket.

The reason we feel comfortable in the presence of natural materials has been explained by an interesting comparison with zoos. When people first built zoo enclosures they didn't understand that each animal needed an environment that was as close to its natural habitat as possible. It's called an 'environment of evolutionary adaptation'. Put an animal in the wrong environment and it tended to suffer from stress, hurt itself deliberately or refuse to eat. Humans, the argument goes, are no different. We live in a world that is fundamentally mismatched to our evolutionary adaption – we don't see, hear and feel the things that we are programmed to respond to. **Modern cities and buildings are essentially 'zoos', places that have been constructed as a replacement for our natural environment, so it's no wonder that we often don't feel at ease.** If we take steps to reduce the mismatch – by introducing as many natural elements and materials as possible – we might start to feel more at home.

'When it comes to ecology, I personally think we should try to figure out what the land had there before – what the natural environment would have offered in its indigenous form.' DR SANDRA PIESIK

CHOOSING MATERIALS

If being surrounded by, or being reminded of, nature makes us feel good, what are the implications for how we should construct and decorate our spaces? It's an area of design that's still in its infancy – we're only just beginning to understand the physiological and psychological effects that different materials and colours can have on people. What's emerging, however, is that although design can be very subjective, most people respond well to naturally inspired design and materials that have a strong connection with nature.

Take wood, for example. It's an extraordinary material. It's forgiving to work with, immensely strong, renewable and infinitely beautiful. Trees give us shade and protection, support other plants and creatures, and clean the air. Once felled, timber provides the basis for so many facets of human culture – from building homes to expressive sculptures, warm fires to wooden spoons.

Recent studies also appear to show that wood – when we use it as a material in our homes, offices and other buildings – can have a measurable effect on human wellbeing. Information based on experiments carried out in Austria, Canada, Japan and Norway has shown that the presence of wood has a stress-reducing effect[7]. Environments that use wood as an explicit part of their design – whether it's furniture or flooring, beams or cladding – have been shown to actually lower blood pressure and decrease pulse rate[8]. In some instances, where an interior is almost entirely wood (covering 90 per cent of the room), there is such a calming effect that the experiment concluded that it would be too relaxing for a work space that required high cognitive functioning (but perfect for a spa or GP's surgery, for example).

Quite why this happens, we don't know. Wood as a material certainly feels warmer to the touch than many others. One study even showed that touching wood with your hands seems to cause the body to relax, in comparison to other materials such as stainless steel or tile[9]. Depending on its treatment, wood also gives a space added texture and visual interest, but our preference for it may come from the fact that touching and seeing timber gives people a reassuring feeling of being close to nature. In a recent experiment, which tested everything from skin temperature to blood oxygen levels, researchers found that people working in rooms with lots of wooden furniture and surfaces experienced less tension and fatigue than other colleagues[10].

Using wood in an indoor environment can also help regulate humidity and improve indoor air quality – timber acts like a sponge, absorbing and releasing moisture into the air. The acoustics for wood are also fantastic – timber can both reflect and absorb sound, depending on which species you choose and how you use it (different woods have different sound-altering properties). Timber as a building material also doesn't tend to transmit impact noises as readily as other harder, shinier materials.

Woods wallpaper by Cole & Son.
(See page 157 for details)

WOOD	LINEN	STRAW
BAMBOO	COTTON	REED
WICKER	WOOL	TERRACOTTA
RATTAN	FEATHERS	CORK
SEAGRASS	LEATHER	GLASS
MUD	SHEEPSKIN	PAPER
COIR	BARK	SHELLS
SISAL	STONE	EARTH
HEMP	LIME	SHINGLE
CLAY	COB	SAND

THE BIOPHILIA SHOPPING LIST

SO WHAT KINDS OF MATERIALS CAN WORK WELL IN A BIOPHILIC INTERIOR? THERE'S NO ONE FORMULA FOR CREATING A MATERIAL CONNECTION WITH NATURE, BUT THERE ARE SOME UNDERLYING PRINCIPLES THAT CAN POINT YOU IN THE RIGHT DIRECTION:

1. **Think building and décor** – use natural materials for both construction materials and the finishing touches. Often a natural material used in the structure of a building is so attractive that it acts as its own décor – constructional timber frames, for example, or hand-made bricks.

2. **Use things fit for purpose.** Every material has its own unique characteristics that make it particularly useful in certain situations. Different timbers have different qualities. For example, oak tends to be heavy, durable and close grained, making it ideal for flooring, while pine is perfect for frame construction but, because of its wide grain structure, not as durable when used underfoot.

3. **Aim for a sensory-rich interior** – nature is complex, so recreate an interior that gives you the opportunity to physically experience lots of different natural materials – by touching them, walking on them, lying on them, seeing them, smelling them and so on.

4. **Where possible, use varieties of material indigenous to where you live.** This could mean using native timber, locally quarried stone, dyes from natural plants or locally obtained wool. If there are local, vernacular building traditions or traditional crafts, can you incorporate these somehow? This is an eco-friendly way to procure and use materials, and you'll create a direct connection between your living space and your geographical place.

5. **Keep materials as minimally processed as possible, without compromising on comfort or utility.** The aim is that the material, whatever it is, should be recognizable as what it is, not hidden under layers of industrial processes, which are often hugely polluting.

FUR, ANTLERS AND HORN

There are certain points where natural materials cross over into tricky territory. If you're vegan or vegetarian, then any animal by-products are an uncomfortable choice. Materials such as leather, sheepskin, horn, bone and feathers – which are often by-products of the meat industry – are familiar 'natural' materials used in interior décor but if it doesn't feel right, then don't use them. From a biophilic perspective, the use of fur may have once been one of our only options for clothing and warmth but ethically and environmentally it just doesn't sit comfortably with modern attitudes to animal welfare and the environment. The same applies with any other animal product derived solely for its decorative use or 'sporting' trophies.

WHY FAKING IT DOESN'T ALWAYS WORK

There may be something about the aesthetic experience of natural materials that also taps into a deeper part of our selves. Natural materials – such as stone and timber – are almost infinitely varied, each piece differing in texture, colour and pattern.

We've evolved to be sensitive to how things look. Being able to visually distinguish between materials and make subtle judgements has been critical to our success as a species; deciding whether something is safe to eat, for example, slippery to walk on or fragile to touch.

Humans are fantastic at recognizing and categorizing materials – in fact, we're so good at it we have a pretty clear idea of what something would feel like – soft, hard, shiny, rough, smooth, sharp, gritty, cool, warm etc. – without even having to touch it. We can tell, just by looking at a woollen rug, that it'll feel soft to the touch, or that a stone floor will feel pleasantly cool underfoot. Perhaps we feel more comfortable with natural materials because we can 'read' them more easily than man-made ones? Or perhaps we just don't respond the same way to, say, laminate wood flooring than we do to genuine timber? The research certainly suggests so: in a study that tested how well people could tell between photographs of real and fake fruit, subjects were able to correctly differentiate between remarkably similar images. Even photographs of real and fake fruit that were almost identical in terms of colour, contrast and spatial attributes, could be separated into genuine and artificial. The study couldn't establish exactly how the subjects could tell fake from real, but clearly there were some very subtle, intuitive decisions being made[11].

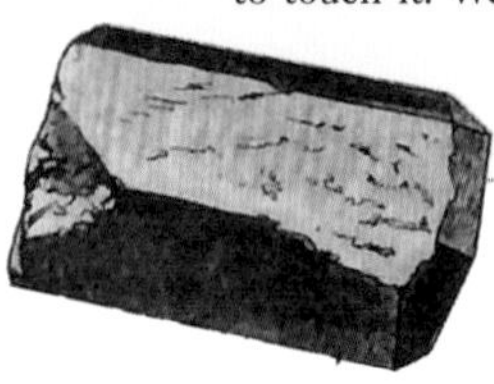

CRAFT + BIOPHILIA

If we want to live in spaces that make some connection to the natural world there's an important role for craft in this dialogue.

Craftspeople have a deep understanding of the materials they work with. These are often (although not always) natural materials. When craft is at its best it expresses something uniquely human and intimate about our lived experiences, as opposed to mass-manufactured products that rarely say anything meaningful. Craftspeople have to know their materials inside out to be able to 'read' them, work them efficiently and create something of beauty or use out of the raw. **Craft has a role in biophilic design because artisans are often expert at celebrating natural forms, using natural materials efficiently and elegantly, or creating connections between natural objects and people.** If we can surround ourselves with objects, décor and designed spaces that celebrate craft – whether it's willow weaving or stone sculpture, sheep's wool felt or carved wooden spoons – we are creating a direct link between nature's raw materials and the human drive to make things from them.

'Nature should make her presence felt in the room in some way'.

GAIL HONEYMAN

THE POWER OF PLANTS

An interior filled with plants has multiple benefits. Alongside their potential use as air filters (see pages 106–107), using plants and flowers as décor has a powerful effect on mood. Studies have repeatedly shown that interaction with indoor plants can reduce psychological and physiological stress in young adults, patients sitting in waiting rooms feel happier and healthier surrounded by greenery, and that spaces which incorporate plants see a boost in wellbeing, creativity and productivity. One 2010 study in Australia found indoor plants had a significant effect on workplace stress including dramatic reductions in anxiety, depression, hostility and fatigue[12]. With that in mind, it's incredible that globally, two-thirds of workers have no plants at all in their work spaces.

There's been a phenomenal surge in the number of young people buying and looking after indoor plants, and sharing their experiences on visual platforms such as Instagram. One 2016 US National Gardening Report, for example, discovered that, of the six million Americans who had recently discovered gardening, five million were in the 18–34 age bracket. The reasons behind this boost in green-fingery are complex: perhaps houseplants are the ideal first 'caring commitment' for millennial renters not allowed to have a real pet; or could it be that indoor plants give people access to greenery in cities where outdoor gardens are an increasingly rare commodity? Young people are also much more informed about wellbeing and health than previous generations and have been quick to respond to the message that indoor plants may improve air quality. But perhaps most of all, indoor plants may just be the perfect antidote to our digitally driven lives. Looking after something living, that needs sustained care and attention to thrive, gives young people that chance to reconnect with something tangible and real – a trend that is being echoed in the popularity of other 'physical goods' such books and craft items.

THERE ARE DOZENS OF WAYS YOU CAN DECORATE A SPACE WITH LIVING PLANTS, DEPENDING ON HOW MUCH LIGHT AND GROWING SPACE THEY NEED:

1. Hang houseplants from the **ceiling**, using suspended canopies, hanging terrariums or macramé baskets.

2. Free up floor space with **wall**-mounted planters, plants on bookshelves, racks, floating ledges, planted caddies and living walls.

3. Make a grand statement on a **floor** with oversized planters and specimen plants, zinc pails, planted log baskets, wooden crates, troughs and florists' buckets.

4. Create vignettes on a **table** or **bench** with plants grouped in ceramic vases, glass bottles and jars, trays, shallow bowls, crockery and miniature glasshouses.

5. Create an indoor **window** garden for plants with glazed shelves, window boxes and glass ball hanging terrariums.

FRESH FLOWERS

Alongside indoor plants, there is an increasing body of evidence that shows that the presence of fresh flowers – whether it's a bunch of daffodils on your work desk or a view of summer blooms – can have a notable effect on wellbeing and mood. A number of behavioural research studies have shown flowers' ability to help improve mood and foster creativity. One 2018 study that focused on women concluded that adding fresh flowers to indoor spaces resulted in a significant reduction in stress[13]. Another piece of research showed that men who received flowers demonstrated increased social interaction and happiness, a finding that expanded on a previous study which showed flowers enhance social connections among women[14]. In a timely piece of research among elderly people, it was shown that living with fresh flowers – with all their colours, textures and scents – not only eased depression but also helped refresh memory and inspired social interaction[15].

A FOCAL HEARTH

Social spaces, especially ones where you plan to relax, often benefit from a hearth or fireplace of some kind. Many homes and communal spaces have lost these focal points, but they serve an important function, one that taps into some of the deepest, oldest parts of our selves.

Firelight and candlelight give off calming 'red' light, which triggers our body's preparations for rest, but they also play a vital role in relaxation and sociability. We will touch on it in Firelight + Candlelight (see page 92) but it's worth mentioning here that focal points of warmth – campfires, open fires, woodburners etc – seem to have an almost magical effect on our ability to de-stress and feel connected to others.

In a now well-known study, anthropologist Christopher Lynn measured what happened to people when they watched images of a log fire on a screen. Some watched images with sound, others with no sound. Lynn then measured their blood pressure, susceptibility to hypnotism and how sociable they felt after the experiment.

The test found that people who watched the fire without any sound gained little benefit, but that the subjects who experienced the visual and audio simulation of a fire had significantly lower blood pressure. But, perhaps more interestingly, the hypnotic effects of the fire, which focused people's attention to the here and now, seemed to help enhance people's interaction with others[16]. In these absorbing moments, the argument goes, we forget our own selfish impulses, feel relaxed enough to drop our guard, and enjoy conversations that are intimate and emotionally rewarding. The very act of making and maintaining a fire is also often a cooperative act – it helps build relationships and gives people a positive shared goal.

It's amazing that these results come from a study where participants simply watched a video of a fire – imagine how much more multisensory the experience is with real flames, the smell of wood smoke and gentle radiant heat. What's clear is that, although technologically we have moved beyond the need for focal points of warmth in our living spaces, without them we are missing out on something that seems to tickle our ancestral bones. Even if we just promise ourselves that, once a year, we seek out a campfire, or that perhaps just one room in the house gets a wood-burning stove, we can enjoy some of the natural pleasures of a real fire.

Colour

COLOUR + PERCEPTION

Among mammals, primates including ourselves are unique in that they have something called trichromacy, the ability to discern reds, blues and greens (most mammals have red-green colour blindness). It's an evolutionary advantage that has allowed humans to occupy a successful ecological niche and thrive as a species.

One theory as to why we developed colour theory is that it allowed our early ancestors to easily distinguish colourful, ripe fruit against a background of green forest. Another idea suggests that colour vision meant our ancestors could read each other's emotions more easily – when someone was red-faced and angry, for example, or blushing with attraction; a skill that would not only make mate selection easier but would also help in the day-to-day business of being a social creature.

Whatever the reason we developed colour vision, there's no doubt that it's a crucial part of our lived experience, helping us relate to each other and the wider world. Colour, therefore, means something to us – we react differently to different colours. Colours make us feel things – happy, sad, excited, frightened, hungry, etc. Marketing specialists already know this, which is why colour is such an important part of branding and product design.

But quite how colours affect us is a little more difficult to establish. The problem is that we all experience colour so personally. On a basic level, we don't all see colour the same way. Some people are slightly or profoundly colour blind, for example. Or, at the other end of the scale, other individuals may have 'extra' colour vision – a recent study suggested that a small but significant percentage of the female population are 'tetrachromats', which means they can see a much wider range of colours than the rest of us[17].

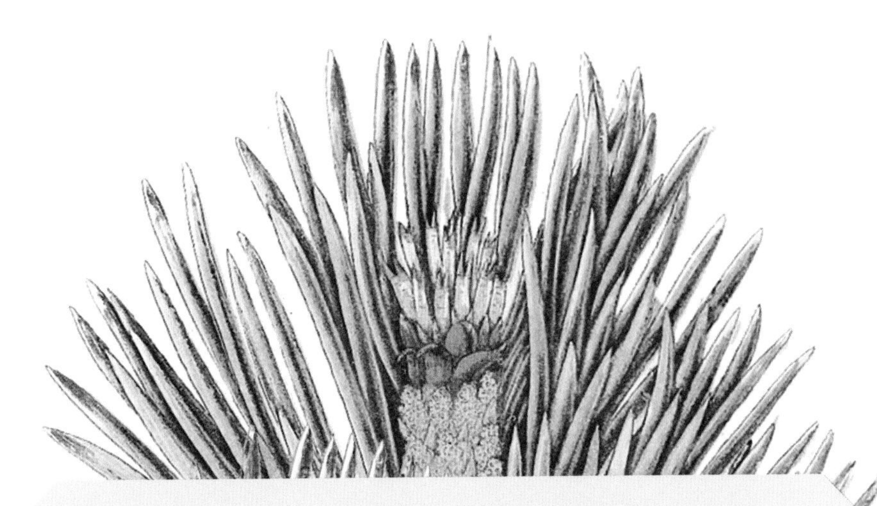

How colour affects us is also tied to cultural experiences. We often feel good or bad when we see a particular colour because it reminds us of something from our backgrounds – a favourite childhood toy, for example, or a sports team's colours. Colours can link to memories of places, clothing, people, books, institutions – everything has resonance so it can be difficult to make universal assumptions about which colours provoke which reactions, i.e. we can't always say blue is a calming colour or yellow is a happy colour.

Colours also produce slightly different reactions based on their 'value' and 'chroma' – value is how light or dark a colour is and chroma is how saturated or washed out a colour is. Think how differently we feel about hot pink versus baby pink, for example, or the emotions provoked by a deep, dark blue night sky and a pale, thin blue summer sky.

COLOUR + BEHAVIOUR

People are hugely interested in colour psychology but it can be difficult to separate fact from fiction. It's been a commonly held idea for decades, for example, that red and other warm colours, such as orange and yellow, excite our emotions and behaviour, make us feel aroused, speed up motor reactions, stimulate competitive behaviour and induce cheerful moods. The flip side of these warm colours, it's long been thought, is that they are so stimulating they can impair a person's performance of any tasks that require careful judgement, accuracy or fine psychomotor coordination, or that they stop us feeling calm and relaxed. By contrast, blues, greens and other cool colours are supposed to have a restful effect and be better suited for relaxing environments and tasks that require concentration and precision.

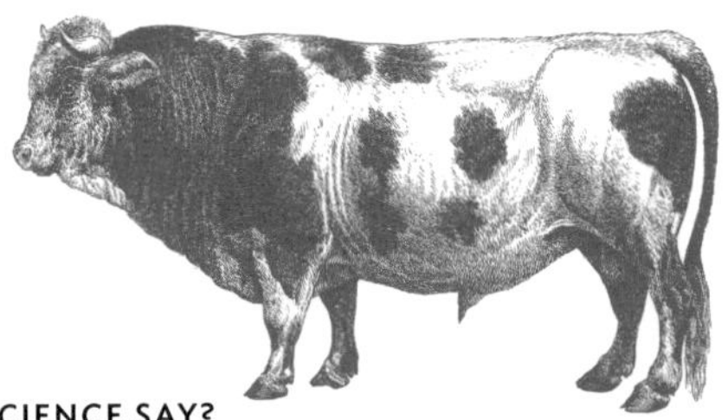

BUT WHAT DOES THE SCIENCE SAY?

Many studies contradict each other and there's still only a smattering of empirical research on the subject. The reality is that we are only beginning to unpick how colour relates to human emotions.

There's been a disproportionate amount of work done on the colour red, for example, but the conclusions make for interesting reading: red certainly seems to be a colour that arouses – in a number of experiments, for example, men perceived women as more attractive and desirable when they wore red clothes or lipstick[18].

In another test it was shown that wearing red sports kit affected a variety of sporting outcomes, making it more likely that a team played competitively[19]. Other research has shown that red may intensify our experience of pain[20], while another study found that people waiting in red rooms felt more stressed when taking a test than those who waited in green or white rooms[21]. Similar experiments have shown red to be associated with feelings of dominance and aggression, to be more attention grabbing, and to decrease appetite. Two separate pieces of research have also found that coloured light can affect heart rate and blood pressure: red light seems to raise the heart rate, blue light lowers it[22].

COLOUR + LIVING SPACES

With so little science to go on, can we say anything meaningful about which colours suit a biophilic space and whether naturally inspired colours can help us feel better in the places we live, sleep and work? In the absence of evidence it's perhaps helpful to take a more intuitive approach to colour, based on how the different colours in nature instinctively make us feel. If we take the natural world as our cue, we can at least try to mimic some of the elements in nature that seem to make us feel good. Think about the variety and ratio of colours in the natural environment, for example. If you were to decorate a space using colours taken from your experience of nature, what would be the predominant hues?

'The world is blue.' YVES KLEIN

SKY

From the pale white skies near the horizon to the vibrant mid-blues of a summer's day, the sky is a rich seam of colour inspiration. It's never just one colour. The most prevalent feature in our natural environment covers a wide variety of hues, values and chroma – the reddish pink glows of a sunset to the grey, almost translucent shades of an overcast day, the glowing orange-blue of twilight to the washed out yellow-pinks of the dawn.

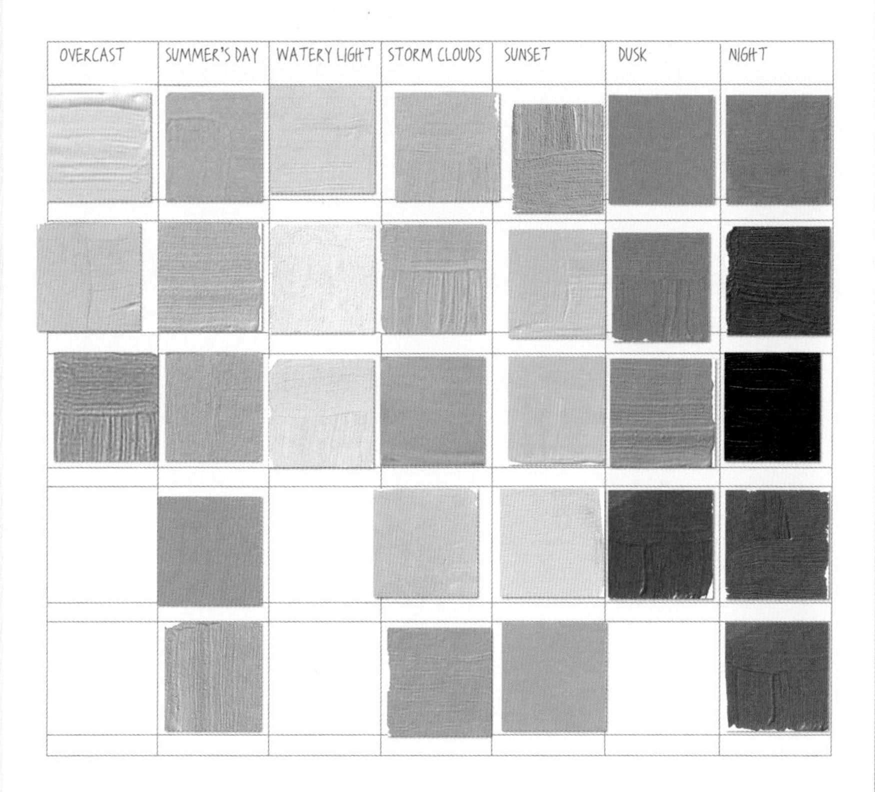

SEA

Because we respond so positively to its physical presence and sound (see pages 132–141), water is also worth exploring as a biophilic colour, with its subtle range of colours. The sea can roll with thunderous grey waves, for example, or read as a calm, flat stretch of green-blue. On a sunless day, stretches of water can be pale off-whites or froth with white-blue foam. The prevalence of blue in the natural world – both in the sky and bodies of water – may explain why it is still the world's favourite colour. A YouGov survey conducted in ten countries across four continents showed that one colour – blue – was consistently picked as the favourite.

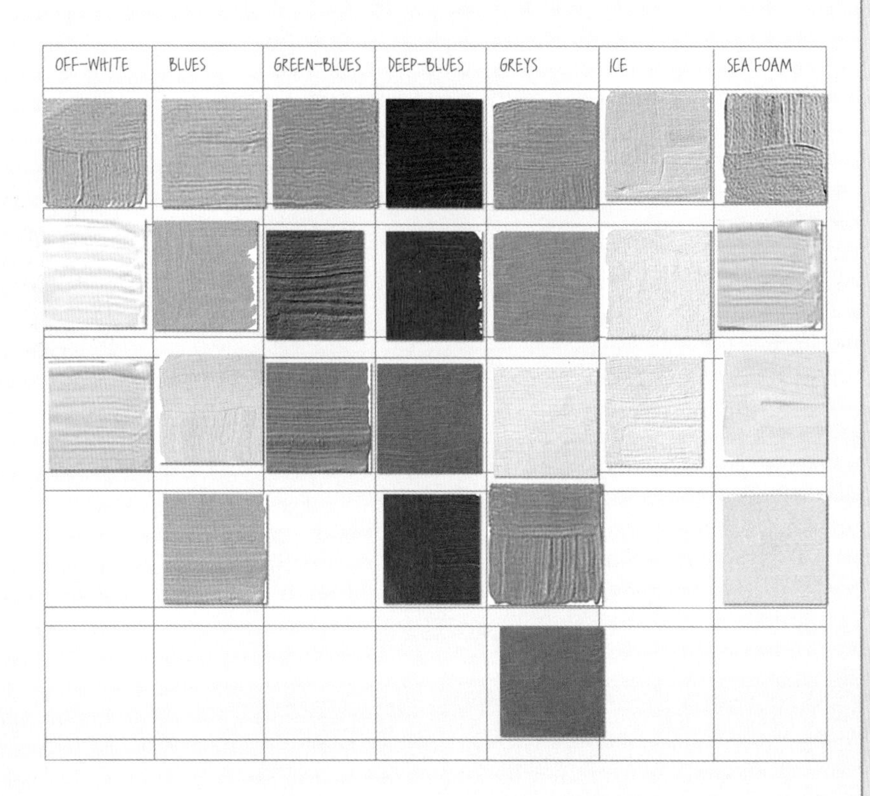

PLANTS

After blue, green is the second most prevalent colour in the natural world. It's the colour of renewal, growth and plant life – a colour we implicitly associate with forests, fields and other fertile landscapes. It's also a colour we find comfortable to live with; scientists believe that, because our eyes – in daylight – detect wavelengths corresponding with the colour green more readily than any other colour, our brains and nervous systems feel calm when we look at green. The cone cells in our eyes are responsible for colour vision and are most sensitive to wavelengths of light around 550 nanometers (nm). This is where green sits on the spectrum.

One theory about why we find looking at green so easy is that our ancestors may have developed a better sensitivity to various shades of green (as opposed to any other colour) because it was vital we could develop a sophisticated understanding of all the plants in our predominantly green landscape. Research has shown that we're predisposed to like the natural greens associated with plant life – exposure to green spaces lifts our mood and sense of wellbeing[23]. Looking at green foliage has been shown to increase attention span and concentration levels, so it may be a good colour for work or study environments[24]. Green also does unexpected things to our brains. In one piece of research, workers who were asked to lift green and black boxes that weighed the same actually thought the green boxes felt lighter[25].

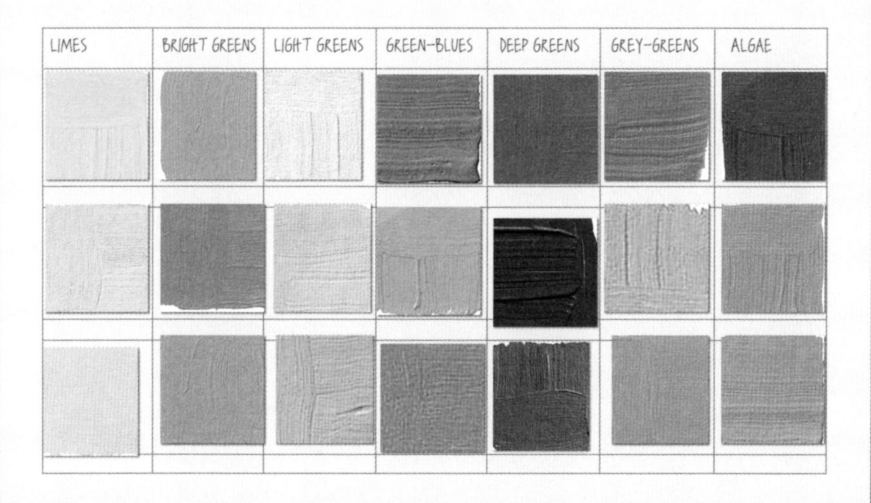

EARTH

The other colours that dominate our natural landscape are earthy tones – the gentle browns, greys, stone shades and sandy hues that characterize the rocks and pebbles in nature – from wood shades to soil, skin pigmentation to fur and human hair – different permutations of brown conjure up notions of rustic living, raw undyed materials such as timber or wool, autumn colours and natural pigments.

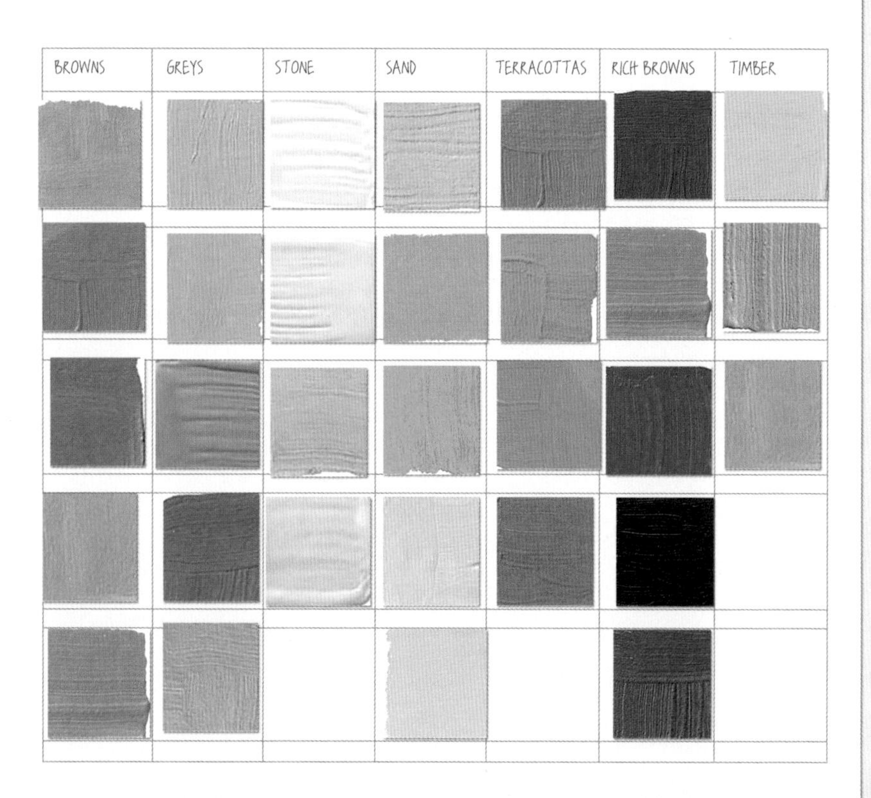

THE WORLD'S MOST POPULAR COLOUR

Interestingly, the world's most popular colour seems to be a combination of nature's most abundant hues – green and blue. In a competition organized by Hull 2017 UK City of Culture, 30,000 people across 100 countries were asked to find their favourite hue from an infinite palette; **a shade of teal** – subsequently named **'Marrs Green'** proved the biggest hit.

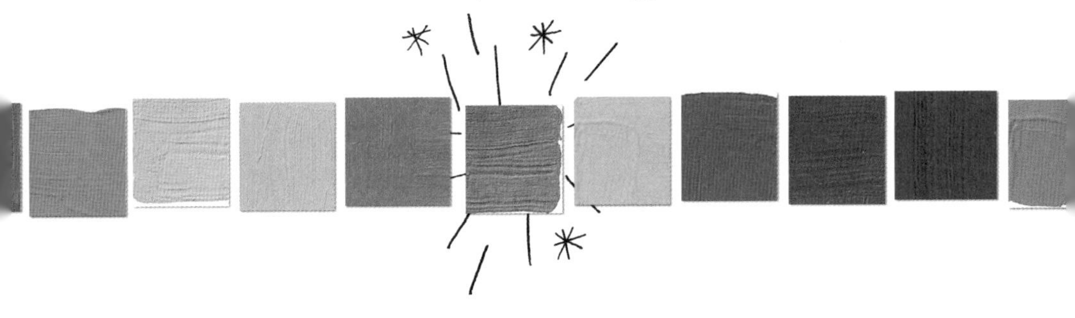

'As the contemporary condition of 'nature deficit' rises in the context of increasingly urban and digital lifestyles, we seek to reconnect with the natural world, hence the current global popularity of the colour green. In these uncertain times, where political and social upheaval has become the norm, we crave the calming tranquility of green and its association with the reassuring certainty of nature's cycles.' CAROLINE TILL

COLOUR + INTENSITY

Colour is complex. When it comes to biophilic design it's not as simple as to say green is calming, for example, or red is an energizing colour. One of the key factors that affects how we react to colour is how intense it is or its 'chroma'. This is particularly important when it comes to large-scale application of colour, such as painting a room or choosing a floor covering.

Studies have shown that intense, vivid expressions of colour increase our feelings of excitement, whereas weaker, washed-out versions of a colour are much more calming, regardless of hue. So, for example, a very pale pink room may make you feel more at ease than a bright, lurid green one. Interestingly, how intense a colour is can change how we perceive other stimuli – one study showed that people experienced a noisy indoor environment as even noisier that it really was when it was painted in lurid yellows and reds[26]. Changing the wall colours appeared to affect how intensely people experienced the same sound.

Reactions to colour also change with age. Research suggests that children up to the age of three tend to prefer bright, primary colours – especially red – more than pale pastels, and enjoy being around vivid warm hues such as orange, yellow and pink. Children also rarely like greys or black. As we age, our preferences seem to change. Adults tend to have a strong liking for colours in short wavelengths – such as blues and greens – and have much less preference for the longer wavelength, warm colours such as reds, oranges and yellows. In our sixties and beyond, our preference then seems to revert back to our childhood favourites – the bright, primary colours, possibly a function of physical changes in our eyes and how we perceive colour in later life[27].

All this would suggest, although it's not conclusive, that intense colours – regardless of hue – aren't particularly relaxing if applied over large areas. And that, whatever your favourite colour, it seems paler, lighter tints are more forgiving for daytime spaces and provoke less emotional, physiological or psychological reactions than vivid hues.

BRIGHT COLOURS

That's not to say that nature isn't full of bright colours or that they don't have a place in living and work spaces. It's a matter of balance. In nature, bright colours often appear in small doses, against a more neutral backdrop of colour. Many different animal species, for example, use bright colours (especially red, orange, yellow or white contrasted against a dark background) to advertize the fact that they are toxic or dangerous, or to attract a sexual partner. Or, in the plant world, bright colours are often employed to entice pollinating insects – such as bees – or other seed dispersing creatures. Either way, nature's use of bright colours is often a strong, attention-grabbing statement.

With that in mind, it's perhaps not surprising that humans react powerfully to strong, intense colours – maybe we're just not programmed to ignore them or find them calming. Which would suggest that, if you want to use bright colours in a living or working environment, it's probably better to use them judiciously if you want a biophilic space. That doesn't mean a room has to be bland; the trick is to find your comfort level by incorporating pops of colours until the space hits the mark.

DIFFERENT WAYS TO ADD A SPLASH OF BRIGHT COLOUR TO A SPACE COULD BE:

Colourful rugs + runners
Textiles – throws, cushions or blankets
Accent colours on wood work
Statement furniture + soft furnishings
Bold lampshades + bases
Bright flowers + indoor plants
Artwork and ceramics

DARK COLOURS

While paler colours can make for a liveable, comfortable daytime space, the potential for dark colours in biophilic design is yet to be fully realized. Dark colours can be richly evocative and create spaces that are atmospheric, soothing and a welcome contrast to expansive, airy rooms. Dark colours can do a huge number of things – they can create the illusion of space, by masking the boundaries or limitations of a room; dark hues also recede, making a room feel larger than it is. They can create a sense of mystery (see page 131) by playing with light and shade and produce dark, cosy corners. The contrast between deep, dark refuge spaces (see page 130) and light, airy social places can be played with in both domestic and commercial buildings, helping entice people through a space and adding a sense of drama.

Dark shades can be an effective backdrop for bright pops of colour and favourite furniture, accessories and antiques. Above all, shadowy colours can create warm, enveloping rooms – perfect for evening and night-time spaces where you want to hunker down for the night. The cossetting effect of dark hues – deep greens, midnight blues, greys, chocolate browns and off-blacks – may even reinforce our circadian rhythms (our body clocks), by providing clear, external cues that evening time has arrived (see page 78).

NATURAL PAINT

How you apply colour is important. Or, perhaps more accurately, what you use to give a space colour matters, especially if you are interested in creating a healthier living or working space. Conventional paints can contribute to indoor air pollution (see page 103); although regulations have been tightened in recent years, there are still concerns about the amounts of toxic substances in household paints, including formaldehyde, fungicides, heavy metals and VOCs (volatile organic compounds). The manufacturing process that goes into making conventional paint can also be hugely polluting – typically 10 litres of waste for each litre of paint (or even higher for specialist paints).

So, if you want to change the colour of your living space, which kinds of paints fit with the biophilic ethos? If you want to buy standard paints, look for brands that have an ecolabel or display a low or minimal VOC content. If you find a European Ecolabel, even better; to qualify products have to comply with a tough set of environmental criteria including embodied energy and indoor air pollution. If a paint has the British Allergy Foundation seal of approval, it has been certified as suitable for people living with allergies, which means it shouldn't contain any irritating ingredients such as fungicides or VOCs.

Better still, look for natural paints. These often use renewable plant-based resins, oils and dyes, are less harmful in terms of air quality, and obtain their colours from natural earth and mineral pigments. There is, however, little agreement on what constitutes 'natural' among manufacturers or which ingredients are more ecological than others – some natural paints use animal products, for example, or still contain petrochemical ingredients but just in reduced quantities. It can be a minefield but, as a general guide, plant-derived, water-based paints are the most eco-friendly, followed by plant-based with natural solvents (turpentine is used as the solvent in eco-paints – it's still toxic if breathed in, however, so you still need to ventilate the space).

That said, natural paints are undoubtedly the lower-carbon, less polluting option. They also tend to be stuffed full with pigments, which gives them a richer, more complex colour finish – one that often changes subtly throughout the day depending on natural light – and won't fade as easily over time. Natural oil-based paint for woodwork also tends to have excellent staying power as it impregnates the surface of the timber, helping create a long-lasting bond.

NATURAL DYES

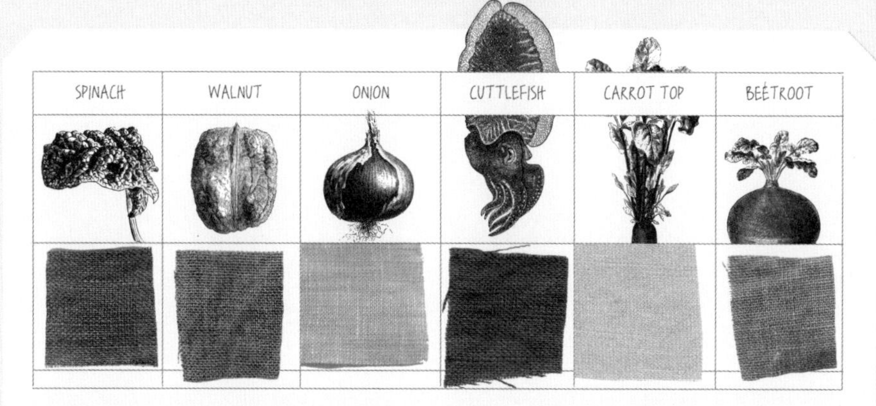

There's also been a revival of interest in natural dyes. Textile manufacture – especially in developing countries – has a poor reputation when it comes to workers' health and pollution. It's also not unknown for people using or wearing synthetically dyed fabrics to develop skin sensitivity or textile contact dermatitis. Allergy to textile dyes, and other chemicals in fabrics such as finishing agents and flame retardants, can cause a number of skin irritations including skin rashes and severe eczema.

As a response to these environmental and health concerns, two greener alternatives have sprung up, which are useful not only for clothing but for any kinds of fabric we might use in our living spaces. One is 'low-impact' dye, which is still synthetic but doesn't have the same amount of harmful chemicals or metal compounds in its composition, and the other is 'natural dye', which uses ancient techniques of colouring cloth using dyes made from clay, mud, plants, teas and other natural materials. The range of raw materials that can impart a dye is incredibly varied – from onion skins to carrot tops, red cabbage to coffee – giving a wonderful, natural palette of colours to choose from. And when it comes to picking which fabric you want to dye there are plenty of options including wool, silk, cotton, hemp and nettle fibre – all of which lend themselves to a naturally inspired interior. Of course, undyed fabric – which celebrates the natural hues of a raw material – has the least environmental impact of all.

Forms + patterns

'If one truly loves nature,
one finds beauty everywhere.'

VINCENT VAN GOGH

We are visual creatures. We often describe things as 'beautiful' or 'ugly' without really understanding why – we just feel it. Aesthetics, the study of how things look and how we respond to them, isn't an exact science but we are slowly starting to discover that humans find certain patterns and forms inherently pleasurable to look at.

In biophilic design, we can use this information in two ways. As we'll see in Views + Spaces (see pages 114–131), looking at pictures of natural scenes can improve wellbeing and that even just fleeting glimpses (or microbreaks) of nature can be restorative. If this is the case then there must be a strong argument for also including natural motifs and images into all aspects of interior design and home living – from leaf-patterned wallpaper to birds on the bedding, artwork that celebrates natural forms to floral designs in architectural details. Nature motifs are everywhere – trees, eggs, shells, flowers, animals, weather, stars, leaves, water, providing an incredible sourcebook to draw design inspiration from. On a more abstract level, there are endless natural shapes we can copy into our living spaces – spots and stripes, waves and meanders, for example, or cracks and tessellations.

Which brings us nicely onto the second way biophilia can use patterns to improve our experience of the built environment. Studies are beginning to uncover just what makes a particular work of art or wallpaper, for example, visually appealing. More than that, research suggests that certain patterns can actually have a positive effect on wellbeing.

These patterns are often those found in nature. The implications for design and architecture are profound. By using natural patterns in homes, public spaces and commercial buildings we may be able to improve the experience of the people who occupy them. Equally, we may also be able to get a better understanding of why interiors and building design often get it wrong – mixing together too many different, complex patterns, for example, which can be disorientating or visually confusing

FRACTALS

Much of the research work on patterns has focused on fractals – these are patterns that repeat the same shape but in different sizes. They appear in nature everywhere – think of a tree limb that divides into smaller branches and smaller twigs still. Lots of things in nature create fractal patterns – leaf veins, rivers and streams, lightening, blood vessels, crystals, ferns, seedheads, even cloud formations.

Psychologists and neuroscientists have both measured people's responses to looking at photographs of fractals found in nature[28]. The results are striking. It seems we are particularly good at visually processing fractals. In fact, our brains feel so at ease and comfortable when we look at fractal patterns, that we find gazing at them actively soothing. Looking at images of fractals that mirror those found in nature, that are neither over-complicated or too simple (called mid-range fractals), helps the brain feel wakeful but relaxed. Looking at natural fractals also seems to engage the *parahippocampus*, the part of the brain that's involved with regulating emotions and is also active when we listen to music.

FRACTAL DESIGN AT LISBON TRAIN STATION BY SANTIAGO CALATRAVA.

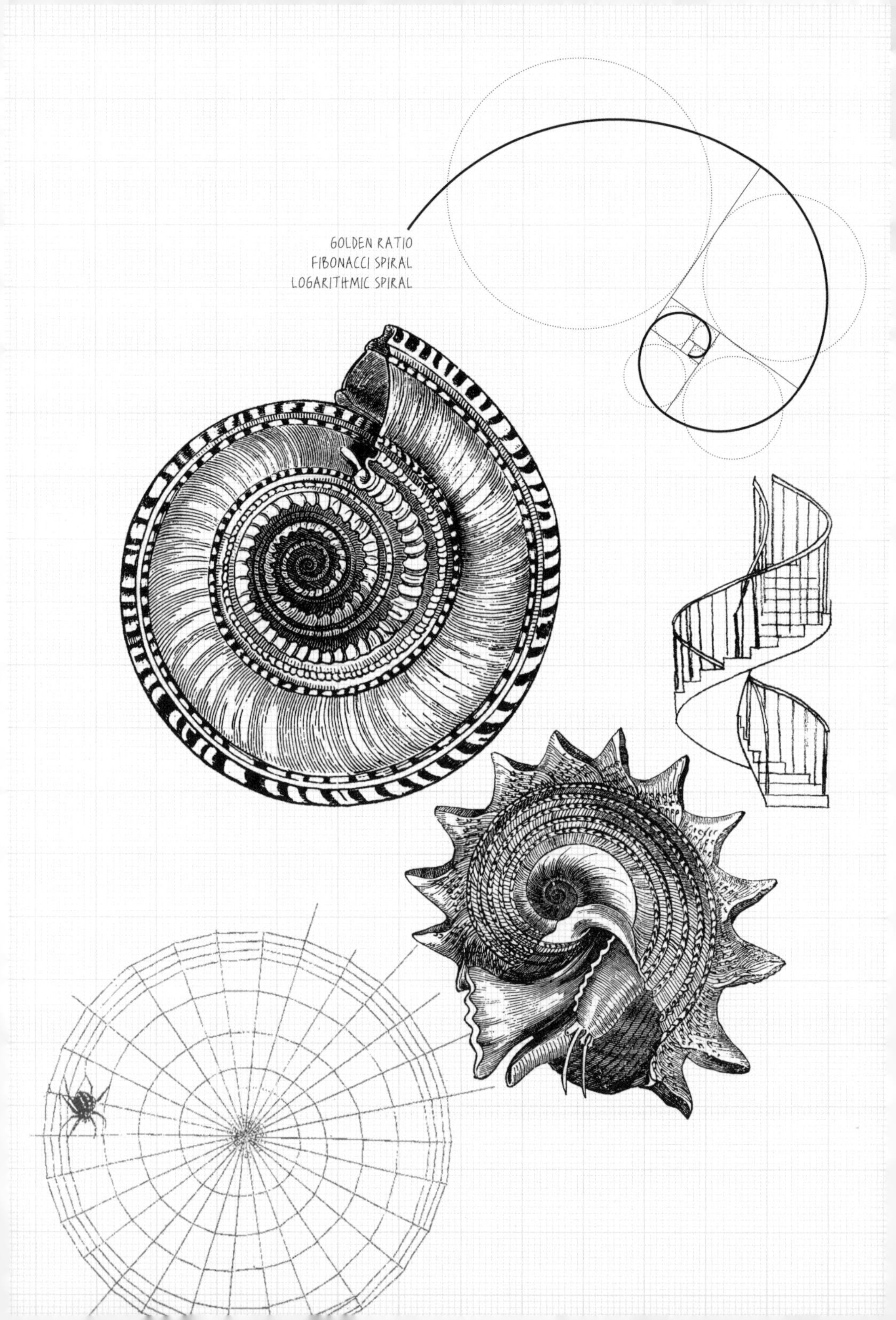
GOLDEN RATIO
FIBONACCI SPIRAL
LOGARITHMIC SPIRAL

SPIRALS

One form of fractal that seems to give us great pleasure is a type of spiral called the 'golden spiral' or 'logarithmic spiral'. Imagine a snail shell. It starts off in the centre with a very tight, tiny curl. Each successive 'ring' gets wider and wider, bigger and bigger, growing the shell exponentially. This type of spiral is found all over nature, in the shapes and structures of many living things – from molluscs to rams' horns, spiders' webs to the nerves of the cornea. Flowers and plants display the golden spiral too – the florets in a sunflower head, the seedpods of a pine cone, pineapples, Romanesco broccoli, the unfurled leaf of a fern. Even galaxy formations, breaking waves and hurricanes are formed in the shape of these fractal spirals.

We don't know why the natural world is full of golden spirals. There may be an underlying physics principle – perhaps spirals are efficient configurations in terms of energy compared to other shapes. But what we do know is that people seem to like looking at them. One of the reasons may be that the golden spiral relates to the golden ratio, the well-known design formula that produces visually pleasing proportions. Rectangles that have a short side and long side with the ratio of roughly one to one and a half (1:1.618) are thought to be one of the most visually satisfying of all geometric forms – we've used it as a basis for design, architecture and art for thousands of years.

Why we naturally respond to the golden ratio so positively is less understood – one theory is that the human eye is capable of interpreting an image featuring the golden ratio faster than any other, especially when it's horizontal.

CURVES

Neuroscientists recently tried to establish what kinds of shape we enjoy looking at[29]. They also wanted to know what was happening in our brains when we did see a form or shape that we preferred.

The experiment asked people to rate pictures of different, amorphous shapes based on preference and measured their brain activity. **The results showed that people liked shapes with gentle curves much more than those with sharp points and hard edges.** Not only that, the preferred shapes produced much stronger responses and activity in the brain. (Previous studies at the same institute involving MRI scans of rhesus monkeys had identified regions of their brains that lit up when they looked at the generous, open curves of a Henry Moore sculpture.)

But why should we like curvy patterns and forms? One idea is that the human brain is highly adapted for processing these particular kinds of shape in the natural world. Shallow, undulating and gentle curves – the theory suggests – remind us of living organisms, especially the movement and shape of muscles and soft tissue. The brain may have evolved to recognize and prefer these shapes as a survival advantage for recognizing prey, avoiding predators and finding mates, whereas we 'read' hard, jagged-edged forms as inorganic or lifeless. Another possibility is that we associate sharp, hard objects and those with pointed features with discomfort and potential injury or danger – the teeth of an animal, for example, thorns of a plant or the tip of a rock. In one brain-imaging study[30], tests found that viewing objects with sharp elements and hard corners activated the *amygdala*, the part of the brain associated with fear. Curves, on the other hand, weren't perceived by the brain as a threat.

They're only theories but it's food for thought when it comes to design and décor. Interestingly, in a different study[31] that analyzed what kinds of architecture and interiors people preferred – comparing rounded, oval and curved features to boxy elements and hard lines, the rooms with 'rounded décor' produced significantly more brain activity. More than that, the test participants were also more likely to say a room was 'beautiful' when it was full of curves, oblong sofas, circular rugs, oval and looping floor patterns.

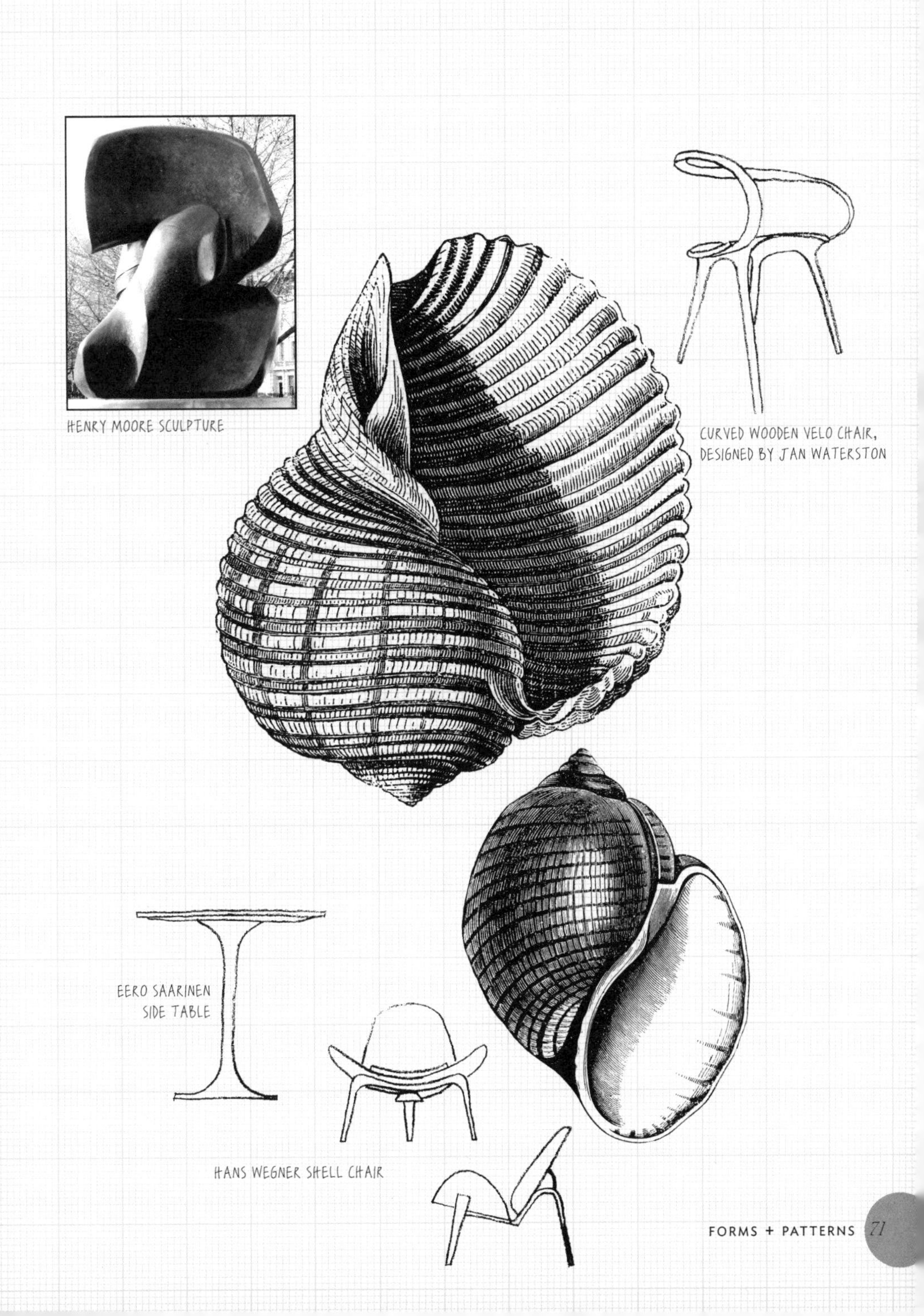

HENRY MOORE SCULPTURE

CURVED WOODEN VELO CHAIR,
DESIGNED BY JAN WATERSTON

EERO SAARINEN
SIDE TABLE

HANS WEGNER SHELL CHAIR

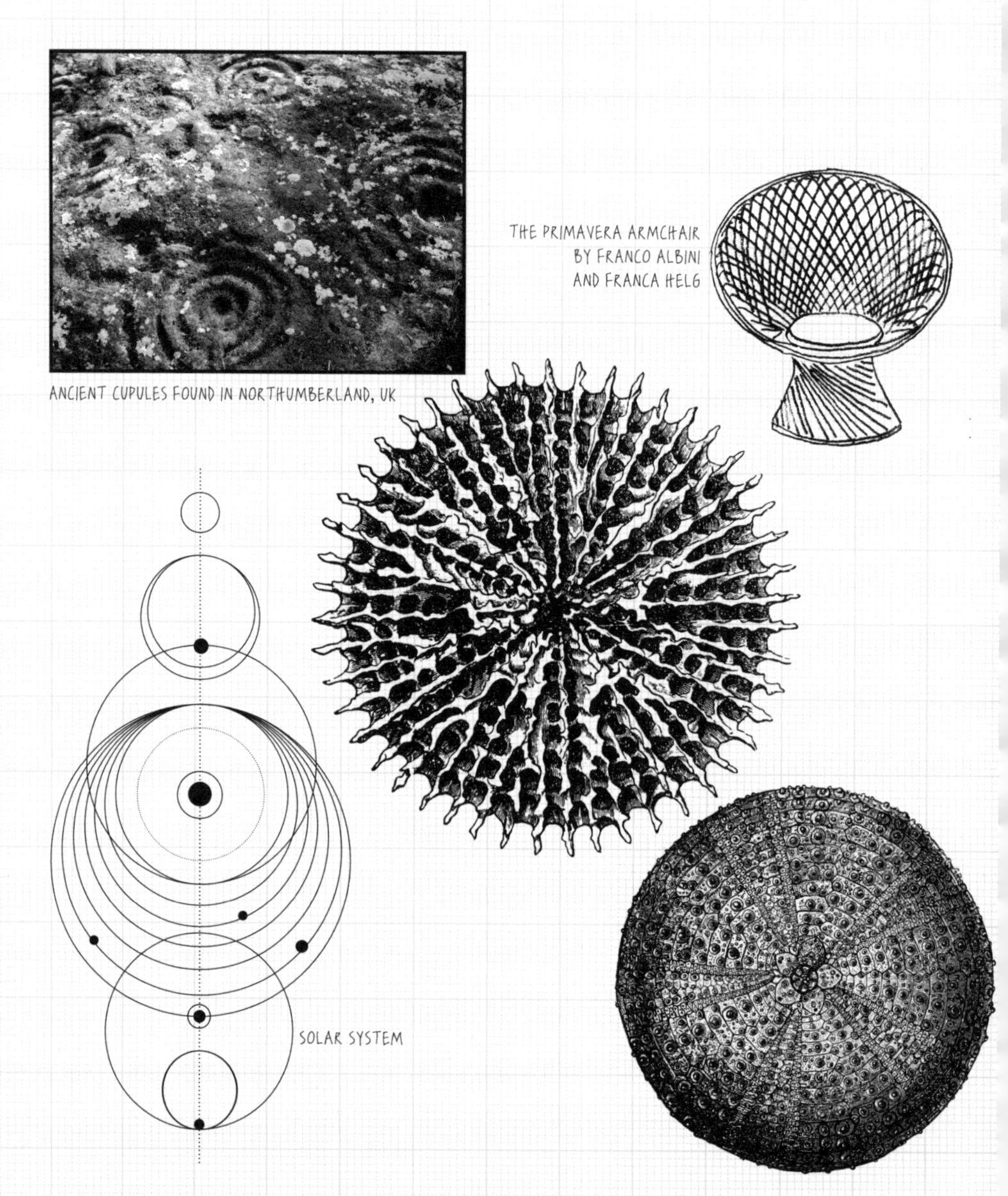

ANCIENT CUPULES FOUND IN NORTHUMBERLAND, UK

THE PRIMAVERA ARMCHAIR BY FRANCO ALBINI AND FRANCA HELG

SOLAR SYSTEM

'...the circle embodies all of the attributes that attract us; it is a safe, gentle, pleasant, graceful, dreamy, and even beautiful shape that evokes calmness, peacefulness, and relaxation.' **MANUEL LIMA, *THE BOOK OF CIRCLES***

CIRCLES

Perhaps no other shape or form holds such fascination as the circle. Some of the oldest art ever discovered are 'cupules', circles carved out of rock faces that are staggeringly old, perhaps even half a million years. We don't know their purpose, but the shape was clearly important for our early hominid ancestors and has dominated design, architecture and symbolism ever since.

There's something deeply ingrained about the circle that makes it a special shape for humans. From not long after birth, babies show a clear preference for circles and contoured lines over straight ones.

Our preference for softly curving forms as non-threatening, safe objects is one explanation but it may also be related to how we read and interpret facial expressions within a group. In one famous study, now nearly half a century old, a psychologist[32] painted the faces of actors black. He then stuck on white dots and asked the actors to act various simple facial expressions – sad, happy, angry, and so on – and made a note of what kinds of patterns the dots made. It soon became apparent that positive expressions were characterized by wide, curving circular-like patterns while the dots on angry faces created more triangular shapes[33]. Our preference for circular shapes may also lie in our inclination to find young infant faces – large, wide eyes, chubby cheeks, round faces – appealing; an ancient predisposition called 'baby-face bias'.

Circles also clearly abound in nature – from body parts to bubbles, tree trunks to tiny seeds – but it's interesting that perhaps our two most important natural cues – the sun and the moon – are also both circles. For most of our time on this planet, we would have lived our lives ruled, in large part, by these two, awe-inspiring natural phenomena; it's perhaps no wonder we're drawn to their shape.

SYMMETRY

Symmetry comes in lots of different forms. Bilateral or 'reflectional symmetry' is essentially a mirror image: a pair of butterfly wings, for example, or the two sides of the human face. 'Radial symmetry' refers to the rotation of elements around a central point, as in the petals of a daisy or a sea anemone. 'Translation symmetry' is the repetition of a shape without changing its orientation; fabric patterns often use this type of symmetry.

So, do we like symmetry? The answer is complex. There have been numerous studies that suggest people find faces that are symmetrical more attractive than those that are more obviously asymmetrical. Work with young children has shown that as early as four months old, babies show a preference for things with vertical, bilateral symmetry, a trait that seems to become engrained by the age of one[34]. Even non-human species seem to be drawn to symmetry – honeybees, for example, prefer flowers with radial symmetry[35], while both barn swallows and peahens have been shown to pick potential mates based on the symmetry of their tail feathers.

One theory about why we like symmetry is that it signals that something is healthy – we, and other animals, use symmetry as a gauge of biological fitness, that someone or something's genes are being properly expressed. Symmetry is clearly important in the natural world. Evidence from fossils shows that bilateral symmetry had already become well established in animals as far back as 500 million years ago and, today, about 99 per cent of animals have this kind of symmetry.

Our brains also seem to detect symmetrical images faster and more accurately than asymmetrical ones and can remember them better. One study using MRI scans showed that the visual cortex region of the brain is more activated by symmetrical patterns than non-symmetrical ones[36]. We like structural regularity. On an intuitive level, this preference for symmetry makes sense – out of chaos we want to create order, it makes us feel safe and in control. It also helps us recognize things quickly and make judgements about our environment.

There is a proviso, however. Too much symmetry can start to get boring. Nature is rarely perfect and our experience tells us that. No face is precisely symmetrical or flower perfectly expressed – environmental pressures, mutations, accidents, experiences, all these things knock the edges off. Too much symmetry and we soon lose interest – our vision stops being challenged and excited. Our relationship with symmetry in the built environment and design, therefore, needs to be more subtle than simply making everything perfect. For designers, symmetry should be the starting point not the end goal – it's a way of carving control out of chaos, creating a structure we can understand and bringing cohesion to a space. But then, it's important to skew the symmetry, not entirely, but with subtle imbalances.

Symmetry is successful in an interior scheme, for example, because it's predictable and comforting; as we already know, scientists have suggested that our brains are naturally programmed to find symmetry attractive, and so in interiors a little goes a long way, bringing a sense of elegance, calm and visual logic to a room. But as with all patterns, it loses its effectiveness when overused. To keep an interior interesting, it's important to employ symmetry only in small bursts or, even better, exploit the concept of 'broken symmetry', in which an overall symmetrical design is lifted by the addition of an extra, random element. Two identical armchairs with differently patterned fabrics; matching vases at either end of a mantelpiece, but only one of them filled with flowers; a neat line of books interrupted by a photo frame or a favourite ornament: all of these are ways of breaking the repetition without destroying the balance. Even in an interior that relies heavily on formal elements for its design, single accents, such as a brightly patterned chair or a striking oil painting will subtly and successfully break up the 'perfection'.

Light + rhythms

DAY + NIGHT

Inside your brain there is a clock. It drives your circadian rhythm, the daily cycle that controls things like sleep, hunger and alertness. This clock regulates itself but is also affected by environmental cues – such as daylight or temperature; if these cues are disrupted it can knock your circadian rhythm out of sync.

Research is increasingly showing that a disrupted circadian rhythm can have a profoundly negative effect on your health. From obesity to heart disease, sleep deprivation to depression, it's becoming clear that many of the problems we associate with twenty-first century living are linked to problems with our internal clocks[37].

So what kinds of things are stopping us from living according to our circadian rhythms? Longer working hours, artificially lit spaces, overheated homes, night shifts, our insistence on 24/7 lifestyles and using technology at night-time are just some ways we are interfering with nature's day-night cycle.

'Early to bed and early to rise, makes a man healthy, wealthy and wise.'

BENJAMIN FRANKLIN

THE HUMAN DAY

For most of human existence, we have lived our daily lives according to the availability of daylight. We would wake at sunrise and go to sleep when it was dark. Daylight told us it was time to be active, night signalled bedtime, lit only by the moon or stars. Light throughout the day would change – from the gentle dawn rays to the full glare of the midday sun, and then retreat again into dusk.

The daytime would be full of activity and stimulation, the evening a time for winding down around a campfire. Studies have shown that watching the crackle and flicker of flames has the incredible effect of lowering our blood pressure and anxiety levels – it appears we may have evolved to enjoy being around fires because they were an important tool for social bonding and community cohesion[38].

Other external cues also kept our body clocks in time. New research has indicated that even slight changes in ambient temperature may influence our sleep-wake cycle[39]. The neurons that regulate our body clock have evolved to monitor temperature fluctuations outside the body – as the day moved towards night, and the temperature cooled, our bodies would take it as a cue that it was time for sleep (see pages 110–111).

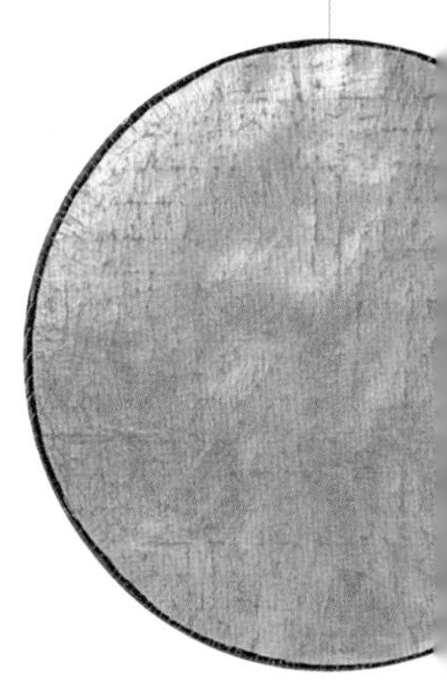

WHAT DO WE DO WHEN?

12.00am MIDNIGHT

2.00am DEEPEST SLEEP

4.30am LOWEST BODY TEMPERATURE

6.45am SHARPEST BLOOD PRESSURE RISE

7.30am MELATONIN SECRETION STOP

8.30am BOWEL MOVEMENT LIKELY

10.00am HIGHEST ALERTNESS

12.00pm NOON

BEST COORDINATION *2.30pm*

FASTEST REACTION TIME *3.30pm*

GREATEST CARDIOVASCULAR EFFICIENCY + MUSCLE STRENGTH *5.00pm*

HIGHEST BLOOD PRESSURE *6.30pm*

HIGHEST BODY PRESSURE *7.00pm*

MELATONIN SECRETION STARTS *9.00pm*

BOWEL MOVEMENT SUPRESSED *10.00pm*

NATURAL LIGHT

We evolved to spend most of our time outside. Access to natural light wasn't an issue for our ancestors – they simply took it for granted – but now most of us live in urban environments and spend our daytimes in buildings lit by artificial light, we're not getting the quantity or quality of natural light we need. In one recent study, one third of Canadian workers reported having no windows at work at all[40]. And, it's not just adults – three quarters of UK kids spend less time outside than prison inmates, with a fifth not playing outside on an average day.

Adding lots of glazing to a building isn't always the answer, however. Full sunlight can be dazzling and create too much heat; sometimes what you need is indirect light (such as reflected light) or filtered sources of natural light (like frosted glass). You can also tweak your routine to make the most of daylight hours.

HOW TO GET MORE NATURAL LIGHT

Architectural

CLERESTORIES

Windows high up in a wall, above eye-level, that let in natural light without compromising privacy. Positioned under a roof overhang they can also reduce glare.

LIGHT SHELVES

Platforms or ledges that sit under a window and bounce light deep into a room. Painting the eaves can have a similar effect.

ROOF WINDOWS

Either fixed (skylights) or pivoted to open, overhead windows allow twice as much light in as vertical windows, without taking up valuable wall space.

LIGHT TUNNELS

Pipes that take light from the roof, through the rafters, and diffuse it into a room or corridor. Great for spaces without existing windows.

INTERNAL COURTYARDS

If you're lucky enough to be designing from scratch, or planning a full remodel, an internal courtyard can create an oasis of light directly in the heart of the home and form a sheltered spot for sitting out. Even if it's only big enough to accommodate a specimen tree or small planted area, it gives you natural light and access to greenery from multiple rooms and angles.

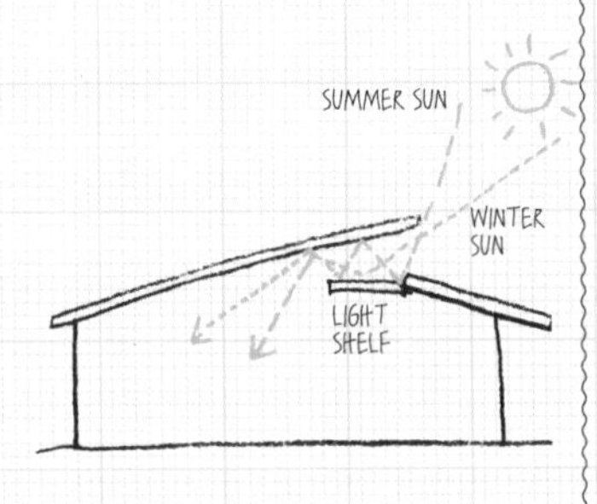

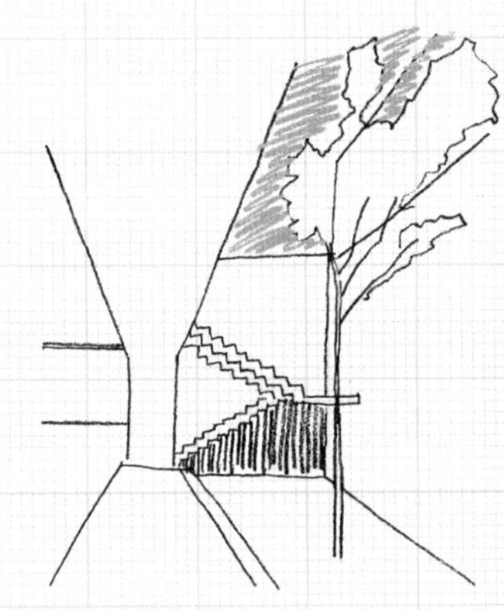

GLAZED STRUCTURAL SURFACES

Increasingly architects are replacing solid walls, extensions, ceilings and floors with structural glass to allow light to filter through.

Anything that creates a visual barrier – a screen, partition or internal door – can be glazed to minimize its impact – glass bricks and partitions, glass roof tiles, glazed and French doors are all ways to allow light to travel through internal spaces.

Large sections of glazing are useful if they're north facing (in the northern hemisphere), as they receive the most uniform daylight throughout the day and don't suffer from issues with full glare.

If windows do face south, and there's too much bright sunlight, place shrubs or planters outside the windows, or use internal, translucent blinds which can address the problem without significantly reducing light levels.

Structural glass is almost infinite in its possibilities and works well on both period and contemporary buildings. Architects can play with form and light with devices such as glass facades, glass box extensions, structural glass 'bridges', oval windows or window boxes, glass ceilings, structural glass floors, frameless windows, glass links between rooms or outbuildings, glass balconies, glass side returns and glass staircases.

Decorative

PAINT COLOUR

Lightening up a living space isn't as simple as painting everything in your house brilliant white. If you face north, for example, and want to paint a space a light colour, choose off-whites with a hint of warmth to prevent the space feeling too chilly, while south-facing rooms can take cooler whites and light off-greys. Think about the hues and strength of colour you use in the home – use the Colour section on pages 42–61 to get more ideas about biophilic colour.

CLUTTER

Too much stuff can be a light stealer. Give furnishings and décor plenty of room to breathe by not overcrowding a space, seek out effective storage systems, and keep your living and relaxing spaces as tidy as possible.

FLOOR COVERINGS

If you need more light in an internal space, think about using pale timber (such as limed oak), painted floorboards, bright linoleum, pale natural floorings, light colour stone or light wool carpets.

MIRRORS

Very shiny surfaces reflect almost all the natural light that hits them. The light bounces back at the same angle it came from, so if the light source is right in front of a mirror, it bounces straight back. If the light comes from a 45-degree angle to the left, it'll bounce off at a 45-degree angle to the right. Understanding how mirrors reflect light means you can play with them to either reflect a natural view from the outside, or direct natural light into dark areas of a room.

WINDOW TREATMENTS

Heavy curtains can help a room feel 'night-timey', especially if street lights are a problem. If you do have heavy drapes, however, make sure they are well drawn back in the daytime and steer clear of light-blocking elements such as pelmets if a room already lacks light. Lighter window treatments such as Roman blinds, louvred shutters and sheers are great for day rooms, or if light pollution isn't an issue, 'naked' windows (without any cover) are ideal if a space isn't overlooked.

Behavioural

MAXIMIZE YOUR EXPOSURE TO DAYLIGHT DURING THE DAY

Move your desk next to the window, grab a window-seat on the bus, walk to work or school, get outside at lunchtime or exercise outdoors instead of the gym. Research has shown that morning light – between 8am and midday – is particularly beneficial[41] (see pages 96–97).

GET OUTSIDE EVEN IF IT'S OVERCAST

Even the dullest day is far brighter, in terms of light levels, than indoor lighting. Lighting is measured in lux. Outside, the average lux levels are roughly:

FULL SUNLIGHT 100,000
DAYLIGHT 10,000
OVERCAST DAY 1,000
TWILIGHT 10

In comparison, most indoor spaces – whether they're classrooms or offices, homes or hospitals – are between 200 and 500 lux. That's somewhere between a very overcast day and twilight. No wonder we're all feeling enervated.

DO LIGHT BOXES WORK?

Some people say that using a light box – a device that blasts out strong, white or blue light can help counteract some of the negative effects associated with lack of natural daylight, such as SAD (seasonal affective disorder) or sleep deprivation. The research is currently inconclusive and health organizations such as the NHS and MIND as yet don't endorse light therapy due to lack of evidence of its efficacy. If it works for you, however, use it.

ARTIFICIAL + DYNAMIC LIGHT

Daylight isn't the same throughout the day. It's dynamic; it fluctuates in brightness and produces different patterns of shade. Where you live in the world will affect the length and intensity of the daylight hours, as will the time of year, while climatic factors such as cloud cover affect the strength of daylight almost minute by minute. Time of day changes light levels too – from the gentle illumination of first light, to the brightness of midday. Sunset and dusk also produce their own palettes of tints and shades.

Natural light varies in colour, from bright, blue-rich light during daylight hours to soft, red-based light in the evenings. The daytime blue light tells our bodies it's time to be wide awake and busy, the redder evening light triggers our natural urge to relax and get ready for sleep.

Environmental factors can also affect how light behaves – trees and plants create dappled shade, water ripples reflect and refract light, or a covering of snow gives a blast of light on a dull winter day; as humans we are used to light being not a static, one-setting switch, but a glorious, shape-shifting, dynamic display. Our bodies and our minds are tuned to these variations and rhythms, affecting our wellbeing, mood and energy levels.

In comparison, artificial indoor lighting seems a poor substitute. Most indoor lighting – whether it's a side lamp or a spotlight – only emits one narrow band of coloured light. Most LED lights and fluorescents, for example, mimic blue-rich daylight, while traditional incandescent bulbs and halogen bulbs tend to give out red-rich 'evening' light. Screens and devices also give out blue light, which is why they interfere with feelings of sleepiness if we use them at night (see pages 96–97).

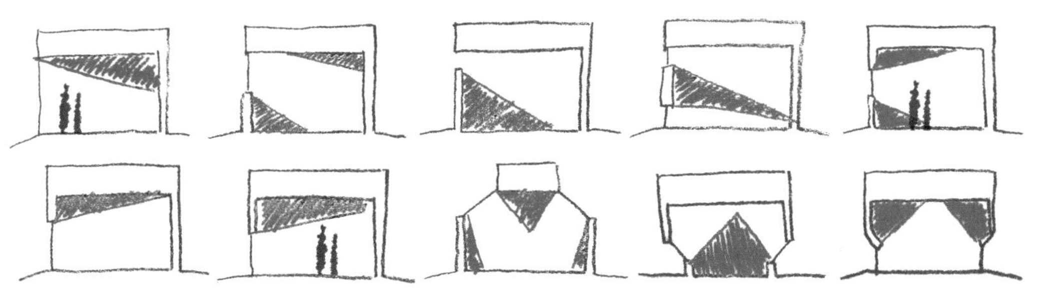

'Architects in planning rooms today have forgotten their faith in natural light. Depending on the touch of a finger to a switch, they are satisfied with static light and forget the endlessly changing qualities of natural light, in which a room is a different room every second of the day.' LOUIS KAHN

Blue day, red night

If we stick to a general rule of blue light in the day and red-based light in the evenings, we can start to help mimic dynamic light in the home.

A great deal of research is going into new light sources that copy the intensity and colour of natural light as it changes through the day – the Night Shift feature on iPhones and iPads, for example, uses the clock and geolocation of your device to determine the time of sunset and then adjust the colours of your display to the warmer end of the spectrum.

Specialist areas of design – such as 'human centric lighting' – are also teaching us how to maximize our experience of artificial light and developing dynamic lighting systems that work by mixing output from cool and warm lights to change the colour temperature and intensity of the light throughout the day.

LIGHTING AT HOME + WORK

ON A DOMESTIC SCALE, THERE ARE LOTS OF THINGS YOU CAN DO TO IMPROVE YOUR RELATIONSHIP WITH NATURAL LIGHT AND ARTIFICIAL LIGHTING. THIS IS HOW COLOUR CHANGES THROUGHOUT THE DAY

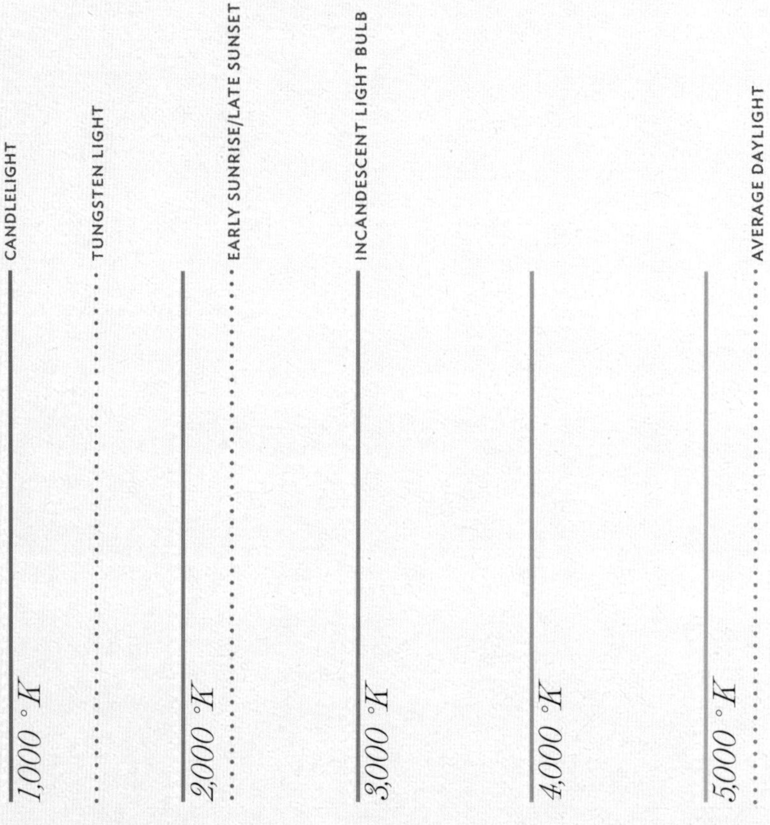

CANDLELIGHT
TUNGSTEN LIGHT
EARLY SUNRISE/LATE SUNSET
INCANDESCENT LIGHT BULB
AVERAGE DAYLIGHT

1,000 °K
2000 °K
3,000 °K
4,000 °K
5,000 °K

Use candlelight and firelight as additional sources of warm, red and orange-rich evening light (see page 92).

Use warm coloured lights for relaxing spaces and evening lighting – table lamps, accent lights and uplighters are better than intense overhead spotlights and central pendants. Coloured lampshades can also change the colour and strength of a lightbulb.

NOON SUNLIGHT

CLEAR BLUE SKY

6,000 °K

7000 °K

8,000 °K

9,000 °K

10,000 °K

As much as is possible, rely on natural light as your source of daytime illumination (see page 83).

Use cooler, blue lights for daytime work spaces, especially if you need to feel energized – day spaces can be more brightly lit, and task-focused.

Look for 'smart bulbs' and circadian LED lights which mimic dynamic patterns of day and evening light.

CANDLELIGHT + FIRELIGHT

What is it about flickering flames that draw us in? Even in modern society, the thrill of an open fire or evening lit by candlelight is too much to resist. When we think of the things that make us feel most calm and cosy, it's often the image of a roaring fire, feet up and a hot cup of cocoa, a candlelit meal for two, or a sociable night spent sharing stories around a campfire that we see.

On the surface, it makes no sense. When we have electric lights and other sources of heating, why do we insist on preserving such ancient technologies?

The answer may lie in our evolutionary past. For humans, the mastery of fire was a key turning point in our social development. As far back as perhaps 1.5 million years, early humans hadn't learned to create fire from scratch but they could exploit a wildfire if they found one, adding extra fuel to keep it alive or grabbing prey that was fleeing the flames. Around 400,000 years ago, when humans began to create fire for themselves, the benefits were profound – suddenly we had access to something that could be used as a tool for defence, light, warmth and cooking. Perhaps most importantly, we think that fires – for early humans – would have become a focus, a place of safety, social unity and story-telling. There's even a theory that our mastery of fire helped the development of language.

Either way, we evolved to need and value fire. **Somewhere deep in our collective psyche, we still respond to controlled fire as something that makes us feel protected, relaxed and sociable.** Firelight and candlelight give out warm red and orange-rich light, which we associate with evening time and helps the body to relax. The movement of flames is mesmerizing, meditative even. It's no wonder that sitting around a fire has been shown to reduce blood pressure and that the longer you sit in front of one, the greater the relaxing effect.

GIRL & MOON
SAFETY MATCHES
MADE IN SWEDEN

SPARKLY LIGHTS

Few light sources can match the ambience of fairy lights. Perhaps once seen as a childish frippery, we've come to value them as a soothing, gentle and endlessly pleasing source of decorative light. While many of us love sparkly lights because they dig into memories of Christmases past, there's probably a deeper, older part of the brain that's being triggered by these tiny lights. Warm white fairy lights tend to mimic other, familiar sources of natural light, whether it's a night sky full of stars or the glowing ashes of a fire floating upwards. Twinkly lights are part of the natural landscape – from glittering minerals to glowbugs – and there's even a theory that our passion for sparkle has its roots in our prehistoric ancestors' never-ending search for sources of water. Either way, there's some ancient button being pressed when we switch on a string of miniature, lustrous lights.

SLEEP + LIGHT

We are not getting enough sleep. Both European and US studies have shown that around a third of us are sleep deprived. At the beginning of the twentieth century, the average person got about nine hours sleep. Today, it's less than seven[42].

Sleep affects almost every facet of our wellbeing. Everything from heart disease to lowered immunity, depression to diabetes has been linked to long-term lack of sleep and, to a large extent, our lifestyles are to blame.

There are two really powerful things you can do, however, to tackle it. Reduce your exposure to blue light in the evening. And get more natural light in the day.

BUT FIRST, LET'S LOOK AT HOW THE BODY'S SLEEP PROCESSES WORK. Melatonin is a hormone that is absolutely critical for sleep. Our bodies produce melatonin when night falls, making us feel nice and relaxed, and ready for a nap. Unfortunately, blue light – which is given out by screens and devices, and some LED lights – suppresses our body's production of melatonin, stopping us from feeling sleepy. It also reduces the quality of our sleep. One study of young adults found that exposure to blue light from technology between 9pm and 11pm shortened their total sleep time, suppressed their melatonin levels, and increased the amount of night-take wakefulness[43]. Blue light also seems to stop the body's temperature from lowering, which is a key part of our gradual slide into sleep (see page 111).

If you want to get a good night's sleep, and you think light may be affecting it, these four key changes can help:

SWITCH OFF SCREENS No screens at least an hour (preferably two) before bedtime. Or, if you can't bear to switch off your devices, dim the brightness or use the Night Shift function that filters out blue light.

WARM LIT EVENINGS For evening lighting, including the bedroom, stick to 'warm' coloured lightbulbs and shades, and keep the lighting as dim as possible. Candlelight and firelight are the most relaxing of all.

SOAK UP DAYLIGHT Get lots of natural light in the daytime. Research has shown that people who are exposed to plenty of sunlight or bright blue-rich indoor light, especially between 8am and 12am, sleep better at night[44].

WILD SLEEP If your sleep cycle is completely off balance, try camping under the stars for a weekend. Studies have shown that sleeping outdoors, in a tent, quickly brings you back into a naturally synchronized cycle[45].

MOONLIGHT

The practice of soaking up the moon's rays or 'moon bathing' – which some people believe promotes healing and wellbeing – is one not yet backed up by science. But it does raise an interesting question – does moonlight have any beneficial effect on humans?

As we already know, we all have our own internal body clock that takes its cues from natural daylight. But one recent study also discovered that we may also have a 'moon clock' or, as the scientist leading the study called it, 'an additional hand on the body's clock-face'.

Fascinatingly, the study found that different phases of the moon affected people's sleep patterns, even when that person couldn't actually see the moon. During full moons, the people in the study took longer to get to sleep, had lower levels of melatonin and slept more lightly than at other times during the lunar cycle. What's amazing is that this natural rhythm isn't triggered by seeing the moon, but rather something innate and ingrained in us[46].

Quite why, we don't understand. Other plant and animal species have lunar cycles and it may be the case that this ancient 'moon clock' would have given our early ancestors an advantage – the full moon perhaps allowing people an extra but crucial night-time opportunity for hunting or food gathering.

The implications for biophilic design haven't yet been explored, but it's an interesting starting point. If someone has chronic trouble sleeping, for example, could being exposed to a full lunar cycle help reset their internal clock perhaps? Or are there any other physiological processes that are influenced by cycles of the moon? One to watch.

Air + temperature

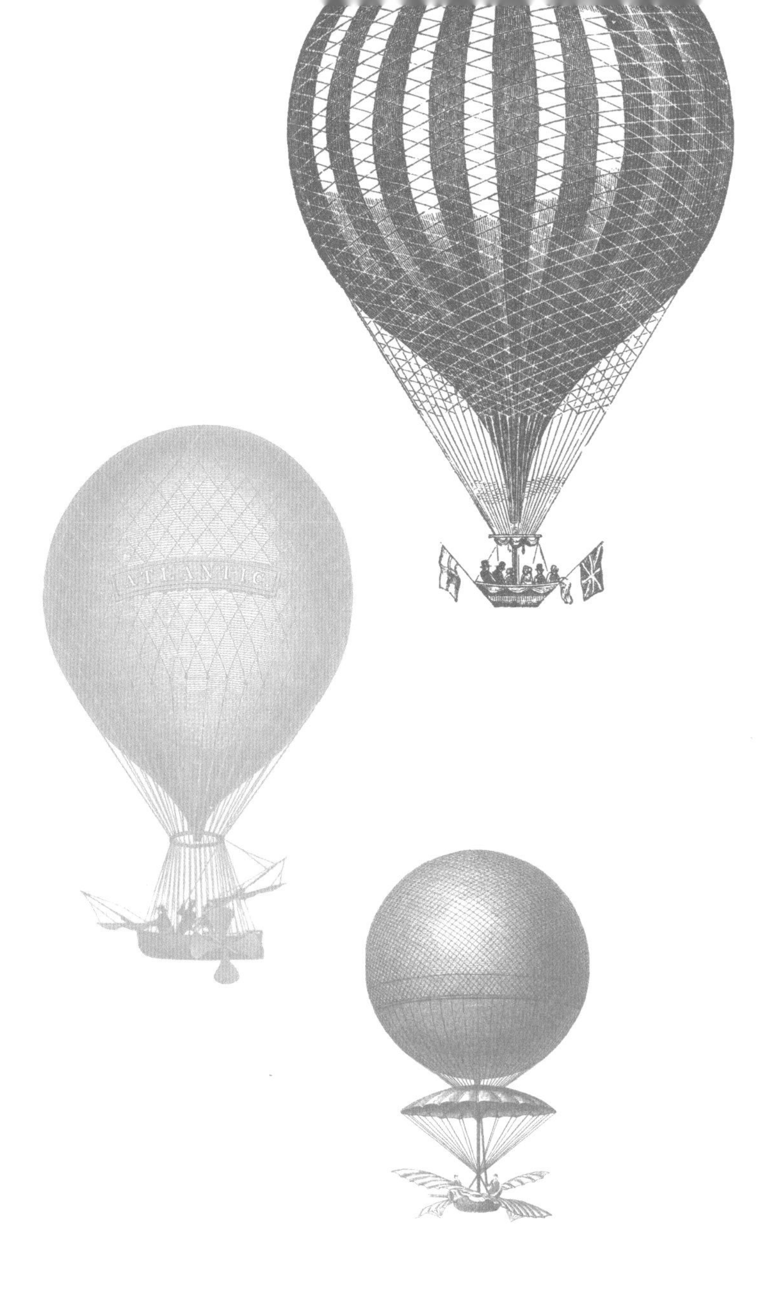
ATLANTIC

FRESH AIR

If you live in the countryside, you'll already know the benefits of lungfuls of clean, crisp air. But here's a dilemma: You work in the centre of a busy city and you want some fresh air. Which is the better air to breathe – indoors or outdoors?

The relationship between fresh air and health has long been understood. We know that certain medical conditions – especially respiratory illnesses such as asthma and pneumonia – are made worse by poor air quality, but there are other issues that have also been linked to breathing in pollutants. From cardiovascular disease to fatigue, foetal development to the onset of type 2 diabetes, it seems an increasing number of illnesses are being attributed to toxic air.

We know we need fresh air, but it's not as simple as just flinging open the windows. In some areas, especially traffic-choked city centres, it is a toss-up between letting in polluted outside air or breathing in stale, equally toxic air from inside a building. Studies have shown time and again that indoor air quality is often worse than outdoor pollution levels, mainly due to our love affair with products and materials that give off toxic fumes, including paints, cleaners, tobacco, air fresheners and adhesives. The Royal College of Physicians, for example, suggests that pollutants can be up to one hundred times higher indoors than outdoors.

BRINGING FRESH AIR INDOORS

BEARING IN MIND THAT WE SPEND AROUND 90 PER CENT OF OUR DAY INDOORS, IT'S IMPORTANT TO GET THE AIR QUALITY IN OUR HOMES AND WORK SPACES RIGHT. SO HOW DO WE CREATE CLEANER AIR INDOORS?

Reduce and remove

You can have a direct effect on how clean the air is in your home. Minimize your use of anything that releases chemical vapours, such as hairsprays, non-eco cleaning products, chemical air fresheners and pesticides, high VOC (volatile organic compound) paints, varnishes and lacquers, adhesives and building materials that contain formaldehyde, such as MDF and plywood. Anything that combusts in the home – such as gas, coal and paraffin – can also produce toxic fumes if they're not installed properly or regularly maintained; these should be properly vented and serviced and you should use as up-to-date technology as possible.

Ventilate

Get more fresh air into your living space. There are three ways air can get into your house or work space; the first is through natural ventilation (opening windows, skylights and doors); the second is through mechanical means (such as in-built ventilation systems); and the third is through the natural infiltration that happens in most buildings (the gaps, cracks, chimney flues, floor joints – anywhere air can creep in and out of a space). In most homes, a combination of plenty of natural ventilation (open windows, trickle vents, etc.) combined with effective sources of fume removal (extractor fans in bathrooms and kitchens, clean chimney flues, etc.) should keep fresh air circulating.

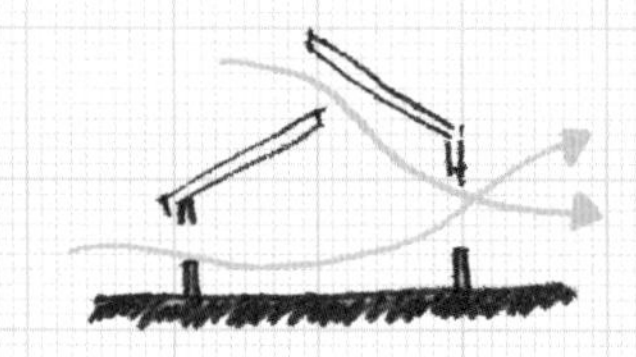
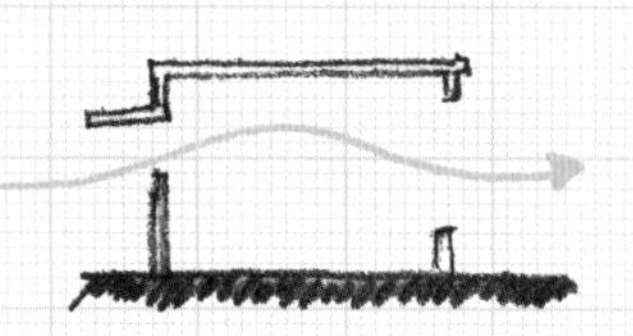
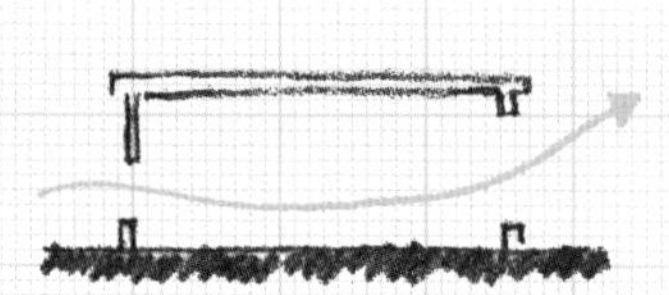

Clean

If you live in a polluted area, and suspect that the air in your building is making you ill, or you're particularly prone to airborne allergies, there are measures you can take to improve indoor air quality.

1. **Establish what's causing the problem**
There are companies and air-quality testing kits that can identify if there's an issue.

2. **Get a vacuum cleaner with a HEPA filter**
These trap the very small particles that other vacuum cleaners simply blow back into the room.

3. **Vacuum regularly or, better still, switch to wooden, lino or stone floors where possible**
Carpets trap dust, spores and particles of pollution.

4. **Grow some air-filtering foliage**
(see overleaf).

5. **Consider an air purifier or filter**
These vary hugely in effectiveness. Look for four things: a good-quality HEPA filter, an activated carbon filter (which removes gases from traffic pollution), the room size it is recommended for, and how many air exchanges it can do in an hour (the more the merrier).

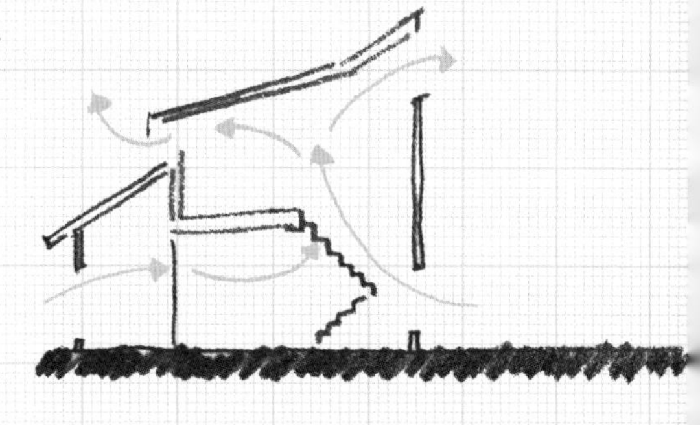

INDOOR PLANTS AS AIR FILTERS

Back in the late 1980s, NASA had a problem. It was looking into the viability of long-term space inhabitation but was wondering how to deal with the problem of fresh air. In particular, how would people cope in a tightly sealed space capsule if it was going to become rapidly polluted with chemicals released by the materials used in its manufacture.

So, an experiment was conducted to see how effective plants were at removing toxins from the air. The results were startling – when harmful airborne chemicals (such as benzene) were introduced into a small chamber containing a plant, the plant was able to absorb the chemicals and leave the air substantially cleaner[47].

Since then, indoor plants have been high on the list for people wanting to find natural ways to clean the air in their homes and workplaces. However, it's worth striking a note of caution. Further tests – done in real-life situations such as open-plan offices – have had mixed results. The problem seems to be one of scale, argue sceptics; the amount of plants needed to clean the average living space may simply be too great to be practical – possibly even hundreds to achieve the same results as the NASA study.

So what's the answer? The man behind the original NASA study, Bill Wolverton, has suggested that houseplants are most effective in removing air pollution when they're used in sealed, non-ventilated spaces, as is often the case in modern, energy-efficient homes and offices. As an interesting postscript to Wolverton's original work, a new experiment in which a devil's ivy plant was genetically modified to absorb more chemicals from the air showed that the new plant was able to take up airborne toxins at a rate nearly five times a normal plant[48].

TOP 10 INDOOR PLANT AIR CLEANERS

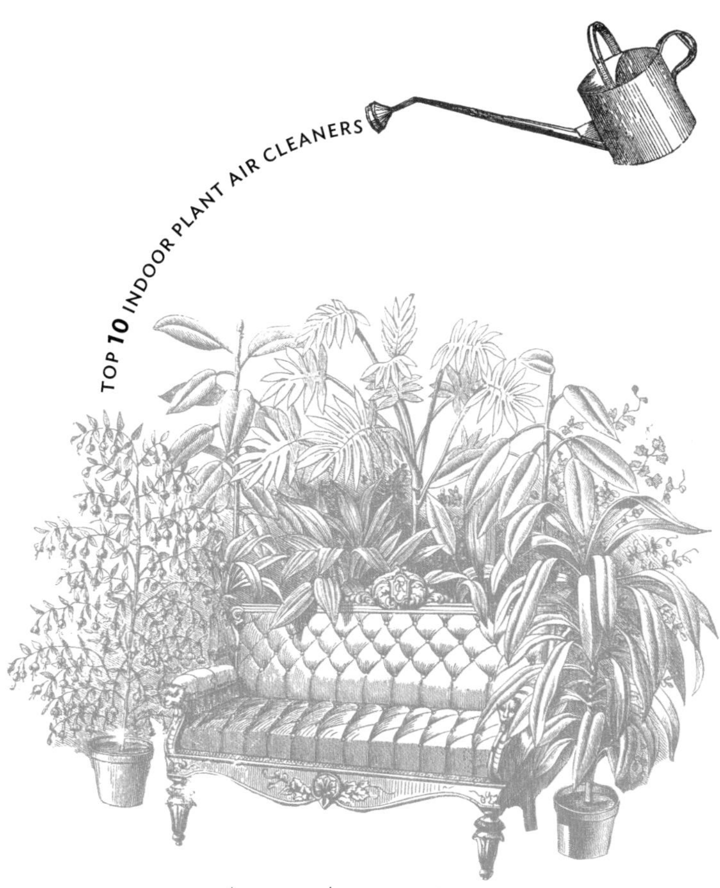

1. Areca palm *(Dypsis lutescens)*
2. Lady palm *(Rhapis)*
3. Bamboo palm *(Chamaedorea seifrizii)*
4. Rubber plant *(Ficus elastica)*
5. Dracaena *(Asparagaceae)*
6. English ivy *(Hedera helix)*
7. Dwarf date palm *(Phoenix roebelenii)*
8. Fig trees *(Ficus)*
9. Boston fern *(Nephrolepis exaltata)*
10. Peace lily *(Spathiphyllum)*

ESKIMO
FAN

BREEZES

Humans like their environment to fluctuate. Slight changes in temperature and air flow mimic the experience of being outdoors but most indoor spaces tend to stick to one constant setting on the thermostat or close off any opportunities for breezes.

Most of us enjoy gentle contrasts in temperature, for example, especially on a small portion of our bodies. It explains why we like warming our chilly toes in front of an open fire or the cooling blast of a fan on a sizzling day. Research has shown that putting people into a work space with different thermal conditions and ventilation speeds seems to have a positive impact not only on comfort levels, but also on how much people concentrated on a task and even remembered things[49].

Breezes are an important element in biophilic living. Alongside their ability to bring fresh air into a space, they do two important things: help your body to cool down by losing heat (through evaporation of sweat and convection) and stimulate our sense of touch. As scientist Jill Bolte Taylor explains, 'our skin is a finely mapped surface of sensory reception' and is 'stippled with very specific sensory receptors designed to experience pressure, vibration, light touch, pain, or temperature.'

'In some cities these breezes are valued and celebrated. Freiburg and other German cities map and protect the wind corridors that come down from the Black Forest and prevent the construction of buildings that would interrupt or block these replenishing flows. These winds provide the cooling and rejuvenating fresh air for the city, sending away pollutants and fostering an awareness of climate.'

TIMOTHY BEATLEY, BIOPHILIC CITIES

TEMPERATURE + COMFORT

DID YOU KNOW THAT YOUR BODY TEMPERATURE CHANGES THROUGHOUT THE DAY? ABOUT TWO HOURS BEFORE YOU WAKE UP, YOUR BODY IS AT ITS COOLEST. AS YOU GO THROUGH THE DAY YOUR BODY TEMPERATURE SLOWLY RISES, PEAKING BETWEEN ABOUT 4PM AND 6PM, BEFORE GENTLY LOWERING AGAIN IN TIME FOR BED AND CARRYING ON COOLING AS YOU SLEEP.

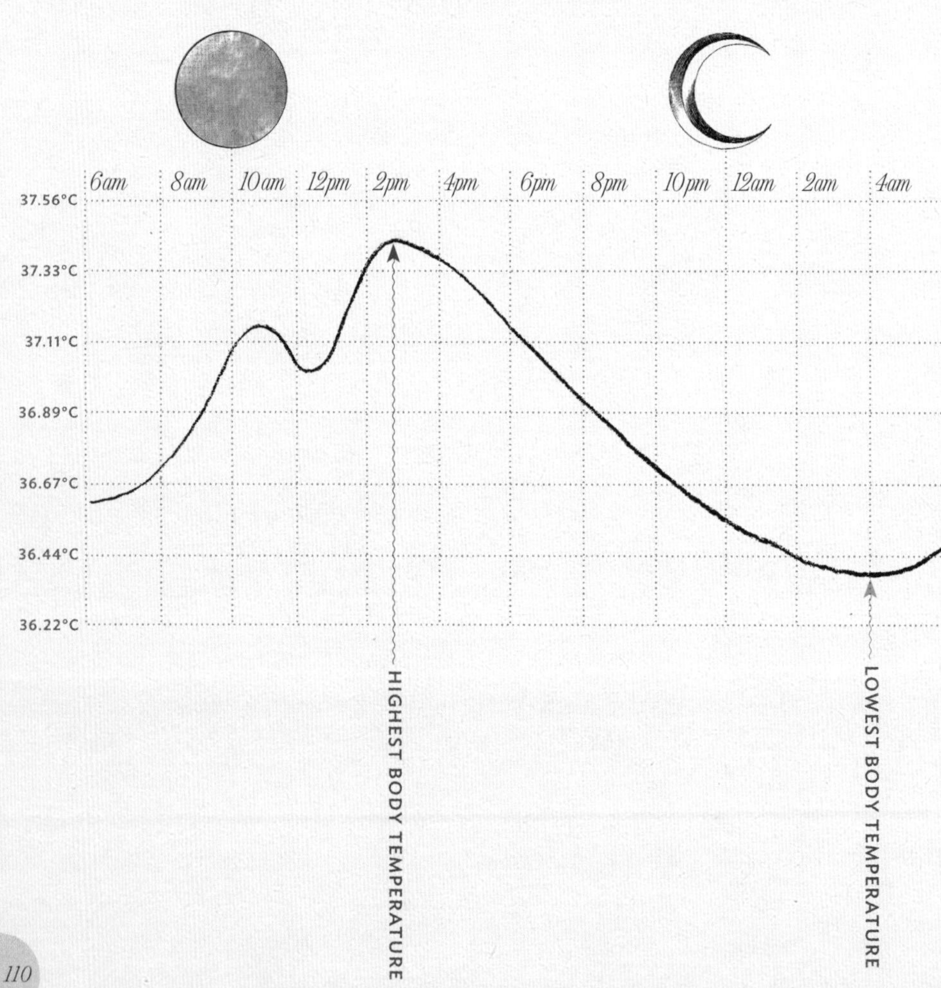

To support your body's natural rhythm, it's important that the temperatures in your home or work space mirror this daily cycle. There's a huge amount of debate about optimal daytime temperatures. How cold or warm you feel can depend on lots of different factors – age, sex, weight, what you're wearing and levels of activity – but as a general rule **most offices should be 21-25°C, while home spaces tend to feel more comfortable at a cooler 18-21°C** (this is because office work tends to be more sedentary than home life).

Interestingly, research has shown that room temperature may affect how good you are at different things – cooler rooms have been shown to help complex decision making and focus during repetitive tasks, while warmer rooms are thought to be better for creative thinking and collaborating[50].

Sleep temperature is also crucial. Most of us sleep in rooms that are too warm to support our circadian rhythm (see page 78), making it difficult for us to fall and stay asleep. According to the Sleep Council, **16-18°C is the ideal bedroom temperature**. When you're lying in bed, your body temperature needs to decrease to initiate the sleep cycle – if your room is too warm it can lead to restlessness and affect the quality of deep sleep.

Cold head, warm bed

It's also worth saying that, while a bedroom can be easily too hot, one of the most pleasant ways to sleep is to have a cold bedroom and plenty of warm layers. When you're trying to get to sleep, it seems that your brain prefers to be cool as long as your body is comfortably warm. In fact, one study recently found that wearing a special 'cooling cap' helped insomniacs re-establish healthy sleep patterns[51] – the traditional wisdom of cold head, warm bed seems to hold true.

ALLIESTHESIA

What's really fascinating, however, is that although we feel generally comfortable in a certain, narrow band of temperatures, humans are innately attracted to thermal changes. It's called 'alliesthesia'.

Basically, alliesthesia describes the fact that our senses will feel pleasant or unpleasant sensations depending on our internal state. So, if a person is chilly and then experiences the heat of a warm fire, he or she enjoys it. But, if we start off from a normal, comfortable body temperature, we don't enjoy the sensation of heat so much. It's the same the other way around – if we are overly hot, and then jump into a cool pool, the sensation is delicious. Leaping into a cold pool if you're an average temperature feels less appealing.

This information is useful in biophilic design because it helps explain the attraction of campfires, huddling against a radiator or warming our backs on an AGA. It also explains our delight at cool breezes or paddling in an ice-cool stream. So how does this translate to home or the office? It helps us understand how we should experience temperature in our living spaces. While it's important to be comfortable, and aim for generally consistent temperatures, it's also important to think about areas where we can enjoy spots of thermal pleasure – from wood-burning stoves to areas of underfloor heating – that tap into our deep-seated urge to huddle around a campfire or put our backs against a warm rock. We can have fun with cool spots, too – unheated bodies of water, marble and other stone surfaces, for example, or fresh breezes from open windows.

What's also really exciting is that research is starting to show some kind of correlation between physical warmth and emotional warmth. One study, for example, demonstrated that holding a warm drink can make people feel more trusting and generous[52], while another piece of research suggested that taking hot showers or baths may help ward off feelings of social isolation and loneliness[53]. Whether these effects are triggered by the fact that physical warmth mimics the experience of being held or touched by another person, or that being near concentrated, controlled heat reminds us of sitting around a social fire, somewhere in our evolutionary past, we don't yet know (see page 92).

Views + spaces

Humans have been around for a very long time. For most of this, we weren't living in urban environments. We were surviving in and among nature, constantly reading, and reacting to, our environment. We are hard-wired to respond to the natural world. We may have shifted to an industrialized, densely populated way of living, but that doesn't mean our brains have lost our inborn affiliation with nature.

THE PERFECT VIEW

Studies have shown that, regardless of cultural upbringing, people prefer views and images of nature. Amazingly, one type of view is particularly popular – the savanna.

This idea is called 'savanna preference'. Research showed that, when people are shown images of different types of natural environment – jungle, desert, dense forest, mountains and so on – they tended to choose savanna-like views. These were characterized by wide, open grassy areas, access to water and a smattering of trees[54].

But why would people be naturally drawn to such a view? One theory is that our early East African ancestors, who made the key move from forest to savanna, enjoyed a survival advantage over other hominid species who stayed in the woods. The savanna allowed us to flourish, so we have developed a genetic predisposition to prefer that kind of landscape.

That's not to say we don't like other kinds of natural view. What's interesting about the research is that children particularly prefer savanna landscapes but, as we get older, adults tend to enjoy a wider range of natural views. It's thought that, as we age, our instincts are overlaid with experience and culture, so the innate preference isn't so strong. We might love a snow-covered mountain view, for example, as it reminds us of the pleasure of skiing, rather than because we see it as a resource-rich, life-sustaining environment.

Another reason why we feel so good when we look at nature is that it has a restorative effect on mental fatigue. When we are focused on a task at work or on a computer at home, for example, our minds are engaged in directed attention. That is, we are super focused on one thing. This directed attention can only last for so long before we need to take a break and recuperate. Exposure to natural views – which engage different parts of the brain and involve different, dynamic things – such as leaves rustling in the trees or clouds drifting across the sky – capture our attention but don't require the kind of sustained concentration that's so exhausting.

WHAT DO WE FEEL WHEN WE LOOK AT NATURE?

How do our bodies respond to looking at views of nature? Research has shown that giving people a view where they can see grass and trees helps them recover more quickly in hospital, perform better in school or the workplace, and display less aggressive behaviour. It's not a new idea – back in medieval Europe, the earliest hospitals were monastic infirmaries; the garden was often at the centre of the complex, its plants and presence a key part of the healing process.

Even short bursts – whether it's looking through a window or even just at a picture of the natural world – seem to relax people, lower their heart rate, blood pressure and stress levels and sharpen their concentration. Researchers in Korea, monitoring brain activity, even discovered that when people look at natural views it lit up parts of the brain associated with empathy and altruism[55]. Looking at urban images, conversely, causes greater blood flow in the amygdala, the part of the brain that processes fear and anxiety.

Just three to five minutes spent looking at views dominated by trees, flowers or water can begin to reduce anger, anxiety and pain and to induce relaxation, according to various studies of healthy people that measured physiological changes in blood pressure, muscle tension, or heart and brain electrical activity.

CONNECTING INSIDE + OUT

At home, build a meaningful connection between your indoor and outdoor space, making the garden or patio feel part of your living environment. Get it right and you'll not only improve the view but also increase the amount of light (see pages 76–99) and fresh air (see pages 100–113) flooding in your home.

Hotter countries, with less rainfall, have mastered the art of indoor-outdoor living. From verandas to open courtyards, outdoor rooms to outside kitchens, there are plenty of opportunities to live life *en plein air*. In more temperate countries, however, if it starts to rain we're often forced indoors, even if the ambient temperature is still pleasant. There are lots of ways to get around this (see oppposite):

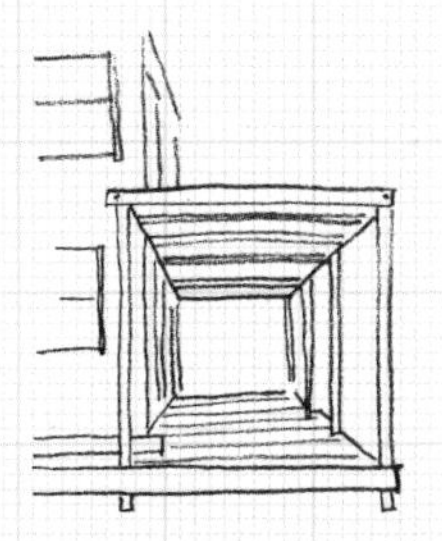

EXTEND THE ROOF OVERHANG OR ADD A GLAZED VERANDA.

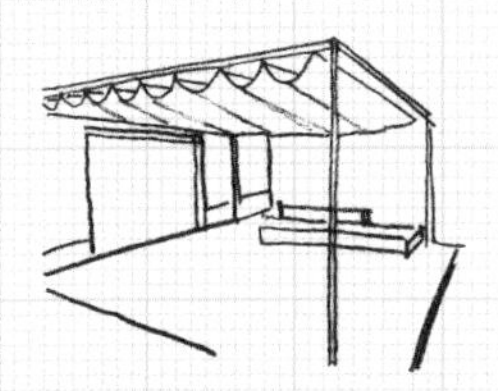

ADD A SUN CANOPY OR A SHADE SAIL FROM THE HOUSE WALL.

BUILD A SHED, GAZEBO OR SUMMERHOUSE IN THE GARDEN.

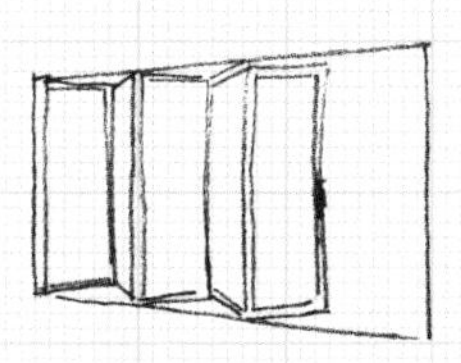

FIT BI-FOLD DOORS, CRITTALL WINDOWS, SLIDING DOORS OR FRENCH DOORS.

CONSIDER A GLASS EXTENSION OR FULLY GLAZED WALL TO CREATE A SEAMLESS TRANSITION FROM HOUSE TO GREEN SPACE.

CREATE AN OUTDOOR KITCHEN FOR COOKING AND ENTERTAINING OUTSIDE.

MICROBREAKS

Even just a fleeting glimpse of nature is restorative. In a recent Australian study, people were given a menial computer task. After five minutes they were asked to look at an image – half the group looked at a photograph of a rooftop garden, the other half a concrete roof. After 40 seconds the groups were then asked to resume the task. The 'rooftop garden' group saw their concentration levels rise and stay increased by 6 per cent. The 'concrete roof' group's concentration fell by 8 per cent. The study's findings suggested that taking these little 40-second green microbreaks – glancing at nature through a window, at a natural image on the wall, or even on a screen – genuinely helped performance in the workplace[56].

CREATING VIEWS

So, what does all this mean for the biophilic home or workplace? If you're lucky enough to have a room with a view, make the most of it – whether it's positioning your desk next to it, turning the sofa facing outside or building a window seat so you can sit and enjoy the view. If you're planning a new space, make sure the windows frame the landscape and that the sills are low enough to allow people, including children, access to the views even when they're sitting down.

At work, the task is trickier. You may have little or no control over the view from your office but, if you think you might be able to effect change, design strategies such as these will all contribute to productivity and workplace satisfaction.

ROOF GARDENS
WINDOW BOXES
COMMUNAL GARDENS
LIVING ROOFS
BALCONY GARDENS
PLANTED CAR PARKING
LARGE-SCALE CONTAINER PLANTS AND TREES
BUILT-IN INDOOR PLANTERS
LIVING WALLS BOTH INSIDE AND OUT
GREEN PARTITIONS

PICTURES OF NATURE

Research has shown that even just looking at pictures of natural scenes can improve wellbeing. Clinical trials suggest that showing patients images of nature, during procedures or in hospital waiting rooms, decreases levels of anxiety and stress. In one Swedish study, heart surgery patients needed less pain relief if they were exposed to simulated natural views (e.g. large photographs of a tree-lined stream) than patients who looked at abstract art or no pictures at all[57].

In one American survey, that looked at art preferences, nearly nine out of ten people said they preferred looking at paintings of outdoors scenes than images of interiors. Favourite subjects included lakes, rivers, oceans and forests. Interestingly, when asked about the season they preferred seeing in a painting, the results were fairly equal – with winter (15 per cent), spring (26 per cent), summer (16 per cent), and autumn (33 per cent).

'Nature is painting for us, day after day, pictures of infinite beauty.' JOHN RUSKIN.

'They are much to be pitied who have not been given a taste for nature early in life.'

JANE AUSTEN, *MANSFIELD PARK*

GETTING OUT INTO NATURE

There's no substitute, however, for getting outdoors. Health studies repeatedly show such remarkable benefits from being in nature that many countries are now investing in renewing or planting urban green spaces; in the US alone the 100 biggest cities spent $6 billion on parks and urban gardens in just one year.

What's amazing is just how potent time spent outdoors can be. One Australian study found that **people who spent just 30 minutes in a green space per week** were less likely to be depressed or have high blood pressure than those who spent little or no time. These 'nature lovers' were also more likely to be physically active and had higher feelings of social cohesion[58]. A Finnish study found a similar result – that **just five hours a month** (which can be taken in several short visits per week) seems to be sufficient to improve mood and attention span[59].

It's also been shown that people who go for a **15–20 minute walk in nature during their lunchbreaks** find it easier to relax at night-time, which in turn improves their quality of sleep[60]. Experts say that highly focused, stressful work – such as staring at a screen all day – sends our nervous system into overdrive, which leaves us feeling 'tired but wired'. Nature, on the other hand, seems to stimulate our parasympathetic nervous system, which is responsible for the 'rest and restore' areas of our brain.

What's more, when you spend time outdoors – among greenery – the positive feedback that your body gets increases your desire to get back outside again; your muscles relax, your pituitary gland is stimulated and you feel both relaxed and reinvigorated at the same time. The more of these 'feel-good' interactions we have in green spaces, the more we are drawn to return time and time again.

However you do it, spending just 30–60 minutes in nature per week – whether it's a city park or a woodland walk, a riverside cycle ride or mucking in at an urban farm – has significant and tangible health benefits.

'Talk of mysteries!
– Think of our life in nature,
– daily to be shown matter,
to come into contact with it,
– rocks, trees, wind on our cheeks!
The solid earth!
The actual world!
The common sense!
Contact! Contact!
Who are we?
Where are we?'

HENRY DAVID THOREAU

DOES FOREST BATHING WORK?

Forest bathing, or Shinrin-yoku, is an idea developed in Japan in the 1980s. It's a clear concept – that spending time in woodland is vital for preventative health and healing – and, on the face of it, deceptively obvious. We all love spending time in forests - surely we don't need someone to medicalize it?

What's fascinating is that what we feel intuitively about the benefits of being around trees is backed up by a robust body of research. There have been numerous scientific studies that have looked at both the mental and physiological changes that happen when we spend time in woodland but two core themes seem to emerge: one is that forest bathing has a direct effect on stress, which in itself is indicated in a number of health problems such as heart problems, blood pressure and diabetes. Leisurely forest walks actively lower stress hormone levels, blood pressure and heart rate more than, say, doing the same exercise in an urban environment. The other theme to emerge is that forest bathing also boosts immune function. It seems something almost magical happens when we're in woodland, something you're probably not aware of; certain trees throw natural chemicals into the air, a bit like essential oils, called phytoncides. These chemicals have been shown to boost human immune defenders, called 'natural killer' or NK cells, which may have a preventive effect on cancer generation and development.

PROSPECT, REFUGE, MYSTERY + RISK

Part of the success of a home environment or a workplace lies in its ability to support human ways of living. A space needs to shelter its inhabitants from the elements, but it should also allow the people who live or work in it to feel both protected from and connected to the outside world in a way that mimics our lives in nature.

If you dig deep into biophilic design, four fascinating ideas pop up, which talk about the importance of buildings that give their inhabitants prospect, refuge, mystery and risk. The four themes can be translated into home and work space design and give people an experience of the built environment that mirrors our experience of being outdoors.

Prospect

This is another way of saying that people like to see what's coming. We have evolved, like many species, to enjoy vantage points, places where we can survey our landscape and spot any dangers well in advance. This is especially true in unfamiliar surroundings, when we are still getting our bearings.

In building terms, this means we prefer spaces with views, especially where we can see more than 30 metres into the distance. Devices such as transparent wall partitions, large windows, balconies, wide landings, open-plan spaces and long, generous corridors can help achieve this.

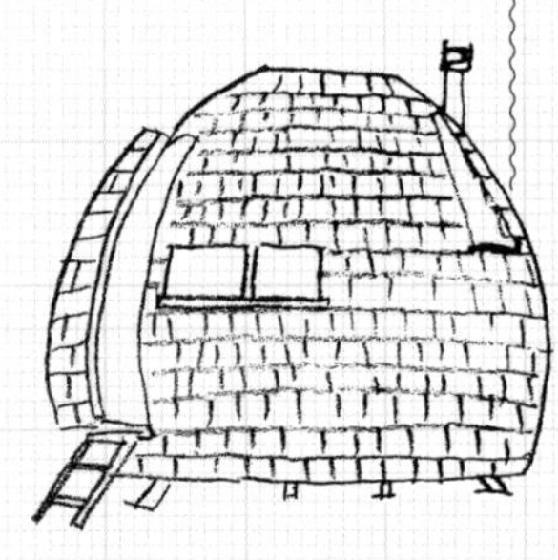

Refuge

At the same time, we all need a space to hide now and again, a retreat from the hustle and bustle. Refuges need to feel separate from their surroundings and offer the inhabitants a chance to get away from the pace and noise of normal, daytime living for a short break. Refuges can offer a number of things – a space to shelter from the weather, a place of privacy, a quiet spot to reflect (see pages 142–151), rest or relax, or somewhere to read, think or be creative.

Refuges can be created in a number of ways. Sometimes all you need is a slight tweak to an environment, perhaps a high-backed reading chair or an office partition. At other times, you might want to create something more substantial – a garden gazebo, a snug or an area of built-in seating that signifies a space where people can relax and be tucked away.

If you need complete refuge, spaces that offer full concealment – such as tree houses, reading pods or sheds – help you hide away undisturbed.

Mystery

So few buildings offer an element of surprise and yet, as humans, we are programmed to relish feelings of anticipation and exploration. Garden designers have long understood the power of green spaces that people can interact with and provide us with rewards for our curiosity – devices such as winding paths, rooms within gardens, mazes and arches within hedges, encourage us to explore further.

Translating this into the built environment could involve curved walls or walkways, which draw people further into a building, or designing spaces that include unexpected niches or recesses. Raised and sunken areas in a building also add complexity to otherwise flat spaces. Playing with ceiling heights adds the element of surprise, especially when you go from a confined space to an atrium, or a narrow corridor into a broad, sweeping room. Even decorative changes can add mystery – playing with light and shade, creating dark corners (see page 58), moving from light rooms to deep, shaded snugs – the key is to provide the odd quirk or fluctuation in an otherwise predictable space.

Risk

This is the feeling that you get when you walk across stepping stones or look over the edge of a cliff. It's that frisson of danger, coupled with a sense that everything is still fundamentally safe. Humans love spaces with a whiff of risk – we like to test our mettle, it makes us feel alive.

Buildings or living spaces need to be safe, but we can incorporate elements of 'controlled risk' which add to the pleasure of a place. Glass-bottomed walkways, high vantage points, stepping over water, infinity edges, passing under water, stepping stones, unpredictable water features, cantilevered structures that seem to float improbably, bridges and elevated walkways, proximity to wildlife (such as bees) – all these devices can add a sense of the exhilaration we feel in nature to a man-made space.

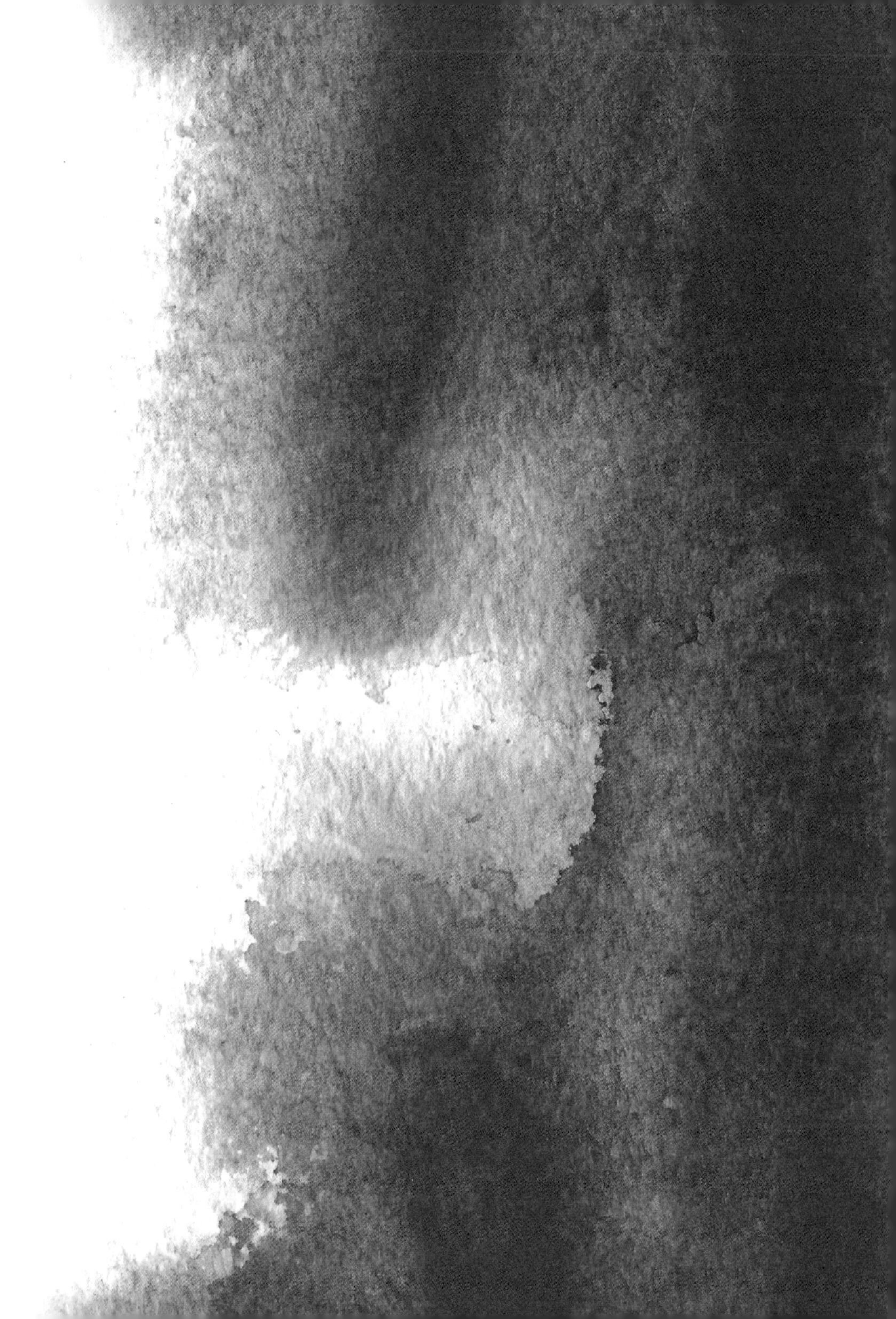

Water

DOES H_2O MAKE US HAPPY?

It's obvious to say that humans need water. Our very survival depends on it. But do humans need water in their living spaces to be happy?

The answer seems to be yes. Research studies have shown that people have a visual preference for scenes that contain water and, importantly, respond positively to environments (both built and natural) that contain water[61]. Whether it's fountains in a piazza or a babbling brook, a small backyard pond or a sea view, it appears that water seems to affect our brains, emotions and physiology in dramatic ways. From reducing stress levels and lowering heart rates to improving levels of concentration and memory, water – in its many forms – has a key role to play in the biophilic environment.

'If there is magic on this planet, it is contained in water.'
LOREN EISELEY

'Water is the driving force of all nature.'

LEONARDO DA VINCI

WHY DO WE LIKE BEING AROUND WATER?

On a fundamental, evolutionary level, water is synonymous with survival. We are programmed to seek it out and make the most of it when we do. Lakes, pools, streams, rivers – our ancestors knew that the presence of fresh water was a prerequisite for life. And even those watery landscapes which don't provide drinking water – seashores – were life sustaining in other ways, providing a year-round source of food and materials.

We still feel drawn to water. When asked to describe the ideal landscape, most of us include the presence of water. In a 2010 study, when shown different pictures of both natural and urban scenes, respondents were asked which pictures made them feel in a more positive mood. Regardless of location, it was the pictures that contained water that consistently scored the highest marks[62].

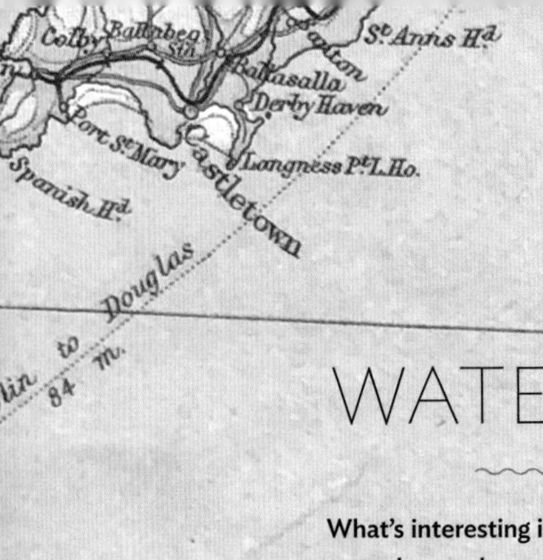

WATER GAZING

What's interesting is that we still don't really know why water has such a profound effect on mood. One theory is that the presence of water – its constant movement and meandering flow – transports us from our usual state of being hyper-focused on a directed task such as watching TV or looking at a computer screen (see page 117) and instead engages a different part of the brain, the one that allows us to daydream or mentally wander in an almost meditative state.

'As every one knows, meditation and water are wedded for ever.'

HERMAN MELVILLE, *MOBY DICK*

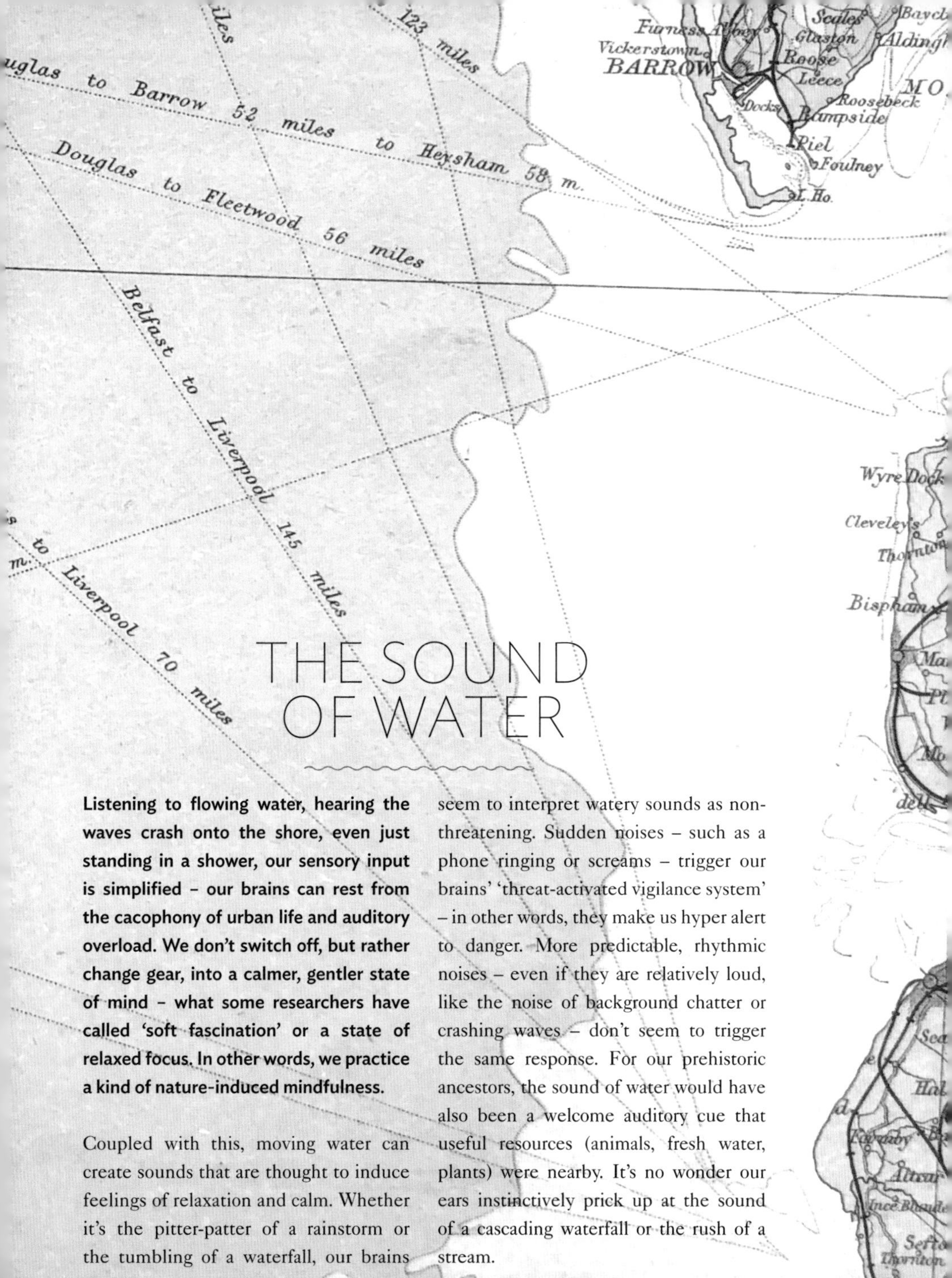

THE SOUND OF WATER

Listening to flowing water, hearing the waves crash onto the shore, even just standing in a shower, our sensory input is simplified – our brains can rest from the cacophony of urban life and auditory overload. We don't switch off, but rather change gear, into a calmer, gentler state of mind – what some researchers have called 'soft fascination' or a state of relaxed focus. In other words, we practice a kind of nature-induced mindfulness.

Coupled with this, moving water can create sounds that are thought to induce feelings of relaxation and calm. Whether it's the pitter-patter of a rainstorm or the tumbling of a waterfall, our brains seem to interpret watery sounds as non-threatening. Sudden noises – such as a phone ringing or screams – trigger our brains' 'threat-activated vigilance system' – in other words, they make us hyper alert to danger. More predictable, rhythmic noises – even if they are relatively loud, like the noise of background chatter or crashing waves – don't seem to trigger the same response. For our prehistoric ancestors, the sound of water would have also been a welcome auditory cue that useful resources (animals, fresh water, plants) were nearby. It's no wonder our ears instinctively prick up at the sound of a cascading waterfall or the rush of a stream.

AQUETECTURE

For decades, architects have been incorporating water features and other 'aquetecture' devices into commercial, urban and large-scale domestic projects. Few projects of any significant size don't include some element of water – from water walls to fountains, constructed waterfalls to aquariums. Urban centres, such as Paris, have long embraced the importance of water in civic spaces. In one innovative new development, for example, architects transformed the Place de la République with a 'water scrim', which floods a huge paved area with shallow, glistening water and allows children to run and splash about on hot sunny days.

Similarly, the floor fountains at Granary Square in London's regenerated Kings Cross region hold a similar fascination – over 1,000 individual jets move and respond to the changing day, from calm and reflective in the early morning to increasingly animated as the day progresses.

For the architecturally ambitious, there are some exciting ways that buildings can be enhanced by either creating a closer relationship with an outside water feature or bringing the presence of water indoors. From interior rills to full-height water walls, indoor fountains to cascading waterfalls, design schemes are becoming ever more adventurous and many take delight in blurring traditional notions of indoor/outdoor separations.

'No water, no life. No blue, no green.'
SYLVIA EARLE

Water

For most homeowners, however, these ideas aren't replicable or practical. Indoor water features have a reputation for being, well, just a little bit naff, but their design has come a long way in the past decade and there are some elegant examples to choose from.

The style of most, however, still tends to be either feng-shui inspired or very contemporary, so if your living space leans towards a more classical or traditional style, there are other ways to reconnect with water. Creating a closer relationship between an outdoor water

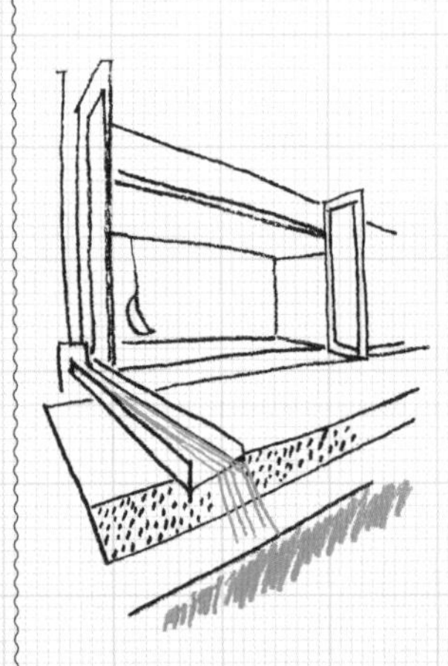

feature and the interior works well, by placing it near or next to the house, framed by a window or a glazed door. Even bathrooms, with their workaday functionality, can capture something of the magic of water and our experience of being immersed in nature – from rainwater shower heads and waterfall showers to large, communal baths and outdoor tubs.

Looking ahead, domestic design may find a way to incorporate water in a more integral way. Designers are playing with ways for buildings to capture and manage rainfall in more aesthetically pleasing ways – roof scuppers, for example, channel rain into a cascade or waterfall, while rain chains and other drip devices encourage water to tumble groundwards in a mesmerizing way. Other designers are developing ways of recreating 'caustics', those pleasingly random light reflections that you often get in nature – say, at the bottom of swimming pool, through a glass full of water or from raindrops on your windscreen.

Imitating water

You can also mimic the presence of water within the home – either through colour (see pages 42–61), pattern or reflections. Mirrors, hand-made glass and ceramics can all create interesting water-like reflections of light, while watery motifs – on wallpaper, fabrics and images – can all add to the mix. From sea foam and curling waves to abstract ripples and crystalline droplets, water creates a myriad of patterns and hues. New York-based wallpaper company, Trove, for example, recently created a collection *Ode to Eau* that evoked the grey, cascading beauty of waterfalls and sea currents.

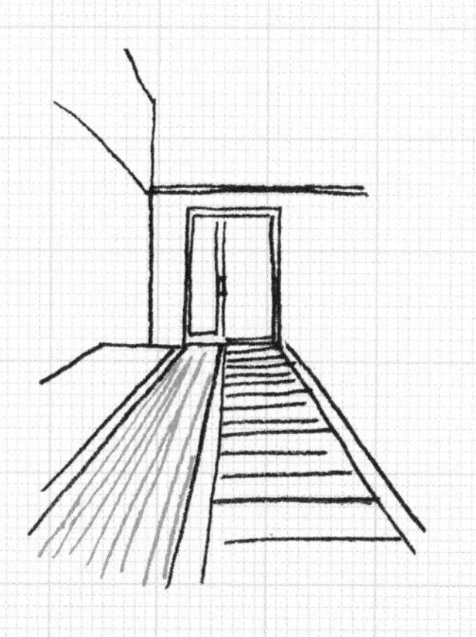

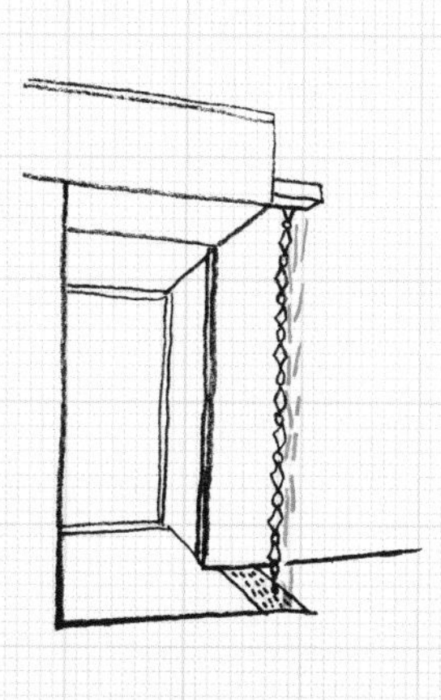

Sound

HOW NATURAL SOUNDS RELAX US

The sounds of a breeze rustling through a tree, the gentle burble of a stream, the rhythmic twitter of the dawn chorus – it's an often repeated trope that the sounds of nature are relaxing, but is it actually true? New research[63] has shown that listening to nature's soundtrack can cause physical changes in both our minds and our bodies.

It seems that when we hear natural sounds it affects the systems in our bodies that control the fight-or-flight response and the rest-and-digest autonomic nervous systems, especially if we are highly stressed. An experiment played both natural and man-made sounds to participants; the results were startling. When listening to natural sounds the brain connectivity of the participants reflected an outwards-directed focus of attention (in other words, people paid more attention to what was happening around them) and their nervous systems showed a more relaxed state. Man-made or artificial sounds, on the other hand, caused the brain connectivity to reflect an inwards-directed focus of attention, a state of mind that is characteristic of anxiety, depression and even post-traumatic stress disorder.

'Soon as the leaves heard the wind's loud call,
Down they came fluttering, one and all;
Over the brown fields they danced and flew,
Singing the glad little songs they knew.'

GEORGE COOPER, *COME, LITTLE LEAVES*

'It is likely that buried deep within the human limbic brain is ancient wiring that springs to life every time we reconnect with these delicate webs of acoustic finery...' BERNIE KRAUSE

NATURE'S SOUNDTRACK

So, what do we mean when we talk about natural sounds? Two terms really help here: biophony – which is the sounds animals make (such as birdsong, crickets chirping and owl hoots), and geophony– nature's non-animal noises (such as raindrops, thunder or crashing waves).

One of the major issues with modern life, especially urban living, is how man-made sounds – traffic noise, building work, planes, phones ringing – have drowned out the natural soundtrack or 'acoustic ecology', often resulting in health problems and stress-related illness. 'Noise pollution', as it's often called, has been shown to have measurable ill-effects – from raised blood pressure and headaches to increased risk of heart attack and strokes[64]. One study even demonstrated that noise pollution from traffic was affecting school children's learning ability and long-term memory[65].

SOUNDS + BIOPHILIA

SO, WHAT'S THE ANSWER? AND CAN WE APPLY WHAT WE KNOW TO OUR HOME AND WORK SPACES? IT'S A COMPLEX PROBLEM, ONE THAT TOUCHES ON LARGE-SCALE ISSUES SUCH AS URBAN PLANNING, BUT ALSO SMALL-SCALE, PERSONAL LIFESTYLE CHANGES SUCH AS USE OF TECHNOLOGY. IT'S HELPFUL TO DIVIDE THE SOLUTIONS INTO THREE CATEGORIES: POLICY, SPACE AND BEHAVIOUR.

Policy

If you want to tackle noise pollution and encourage natural sounds back into the wider environment, it's important to think big. Get involved in creating local policy or strategies for your area – you can affect change on any subjects such as airport noise, transport and road congestion, business opening hours or other noise-generating factors; use social media, volunteer for a campaign group, find like-minded people, talk to local media, organize community events or become a councillor. Campaign for more green space in your environment, whether it's protecting current parks and open land or creating new wildlife areas. Support local green spaces where you can experience biophonic and geophonic sound – urban farms, wildlife havens, conservation areas and national parks.

Space

Change the spaces you live and work in to reduce man-made noise. At home, this could include sound insulation, double glazing, sound-blocking doors, and using quieter domestic appliances. Office life can also be very noisy – the prevalence of open-plan spaces has meant that work can be very distracting, a constant thrum of phones ringing, chatter and background noise. Research conducted back in 1998 showed that noisy, open-plan offices massively reduced the productivity of workers, especially if they needed to do tasks that involved manipulating numbers or words, or writing reports[66].

If you can change your work environment, a balance between open spaces, where people can work together, and refuge areas, (see page 130) where people can either work or think in isolation or quiet, have proved to be more popular with employees. In one fascinating trial, one US design agency, Navy, decided to institute daily 'quiet time' before lunch, when the team agreed to be silent and switch off all access to technology. After four years, the team were almost a quarter more productive and measurably less stressed.

Think about ways to introduce natural sounds into your environment. Water features not only produce their own geophonic sound but they can often encourage natural life to follow – insects, birds, amphibians, all of which can add to nature's acoustics. City life can be rich pickings for wild birds, for example.

Encourage birdsong into your outside space at home or work by providing bird food or shelter, planting fruit or berry trees, installing a bird bath or creating a bug-friendly flower garden, which in turn entices in more bird life.

Breezes (see page 109) create their own sounds. Look into ways to allow fresh air to move dynamically around a space, for example, or through planted areas of leafy trees. Rainfall is another soothing sound, akin to the calming effects of white noise; can you create opportunities where you can listen to and enjoy rainfall from a position of shelter – under a skylight, metal roof covering, canvas, or a garden building for example?

Behaviour

On an individual level, we can all do things to mitigate the effects of man-made noise and find ways to introduce more natural sounds into our daily lives. Reduce your exposure to the ever-present din – turn off the tech, don't always have music or the television blaring in the background, take noise-cancelling headphones or earplugs to work, seek out quiet spaces and find opportunities to visit green, nature-filled places, whether it's a walk in the woods or a stroll around a city park.

'...the rain whispered like my mothers voice,
singing simple hymns and melodies.' JOHN M. HULL

NATURE SOUND APPS

There has been a huge surge in people listening to recordings of natural noises, as aids to both relaxation and sleep. While they don't address the critical problem of our lack of contact with nature, what is interesting is the breadth of natural sounds people find calming and how these digital simulations are clearly filling a void in our lives. Natural sounds that people respond positively to are wonderfully varied – from waves to crickets, seagulls to crackling fires, and even include some of the sounds that we might not initially think of as 'calming' – such as distant thunder or wolf howls. Users of natural sound apps are also widening their application – from improving insomnia and the experience of childbirth or chronic pain, to enhancing creativity at work or helping people with tinnitus find relief.

'Everything you can imagine, nature has already created.'

ALBERT EINSTEIN

References

1 Collaboration for Environmental Evidence. *'The Importance Of Nature For Health: Is There A Specific Benefit Of Contact With Green Space?'* www.environmentalevidence.org/completed-reviews, page 16

2 Ulrich, R.S.. *'View Through A Window May Influence Recovery From Surgery.'* Science 224 (1984): 420-421, page 16

3 NHS Forest, *'Evidence of Benefits.'* nhsforest.org/Evidence-Benefits, page 17

4 Änggård, Eva. *'Children's Gendered And Non-Gendered Play In Natural Spaces.'* Children, Youth and Environments 21, no. 2 (2011): 5-33, page 22

5 Pearson, David G., and Tony Craig. *'The Great Outdoors? Exploring The Mental Health Benefits Of Natural Environments.'* Frontiers in Psychology 5 (2014): 1178, page 22

6 Broom, Catherine. *'Exploring The Relations Between Childhood Experiences In Nature And Young Adults Environmental Attitudes And Behaviours.'* Australian Journal of Environmental Education 33, no. 1 (2017): 34–47, page 22

Habitat: Vernacular Architecture for a Changing Planet © 2017 by Sandra Piesik. Reprinted by kind permission of Thames & Hudson Ltd., page 29

7 Fell, David Robert. *'Wood In The Human Environment: Restorative Properties Of Wood In The Built Indoor Environment.'* PhD thesis, The University of British Columbia, 2010, page 31

8 Nyrud, Anders Q.. *'Is Interior Wood Use Psychologically Beneficial? A Review Of Psychological Responses Toward Wood.'* Wood and Fiber Science 42, no. 2 (2010): 202–218, page 31

9 Ikei, Harumi et al. *'Physiological Effects Of Touching Wood.'* International Journal of Environmental Research and Public Health 14, no. 7 (2017): 801, page 31

10 *Wood in the Human Environment: Restorative Properties of Wood in the Built Indoor Environment.* David Robert Fell, page 31

11 Sharan, L. et al. *'Eye Movements For Material Perception.'* Journal of Vision 8, no. 6 (2008): 219a, page 34

Elinor Oliphant is Completely Fine © 2017 by Gail Honeyman Reprinted by permission of HarperCollins Publishers Ltd, page 35

12 Bringslimark, Tina et al. *'Psychological Benefits Of Indoor Plants In Workplaces: Putting Experimental Results Into Context.'* American Society for Horticultural Science 42, no. 3 (2007): 581–587, page 36

13 University of North Florida in partnership with the Society of American Florists. *'The Impact of Flowers On Perceived Stress Among Women.'* https://aboutflowers.com/quick-links/health-benefits-research/stressless/, page 39

14 Haviland-Jones, Jeannette M. *'The Emotional Impact of Flowers Study.'* Rutgers, The State University of New Jersey. https://aboutflowers.com/quick-links/health-benefits-research/emotional-impact-of-flowers-study/, page 39

15 Haviland-Jones, Jeannette M. *'Flowers and Seniors Study.'* Rutgers, The State University of New Jersey. https://aboutflowers.com/quick-links/health-benefits-research/flowers-seniors-study/, page 39

16 Lynn, C. D.. *'The Psychophysiology Of Fireside Relaxation.'* American Journal of Human Biology 25 (2013): 265–265, page 41

17 Jordan, Gabriele et al. *'The Dimensionality Of Color Vision In Carriers Of Anomalous Trichromacy.'* Journal of Vision 10, no.8 (2010), page 44

18 The Uncanny Power of the Red Dress, Psychology today, https://www.psychologytoday.com/gb/blog/attraction-evolved/201604/the-uncanny-power-red-dress, Page 47

19 Rowe, C. et al. *'Sporting Contests - Seeing Red? Putting Sportswear In Context.'* Nature 437, no. 7063 (2005), page 47

20 Martini, Matteo et al. *'What Color Is My Arm? Changes In Skin Color Of An Embodied Virtual Arm Modulates Pain Threshold.'* Frontiers in Human Neuroscience 7, no. 438 (2013), page 47

21 Kutchma, Teresa M.. *'The Effects Of Room Color On Stress Perception: Red Versus Green Environments.'* Journal of Undergraduate Research, Cornerstone, Minnesotaa State University, Mankato 3 (2003), page 47

22 AL Ayash, Aseel et al. *'The Influence Of Color On Student Emotion, Heart Rate, And Performance In Learning Environments.'* Color Research and Application 41, no. 2 (2016): 196–205, page 47

23 Barton, Jo, and Mike Rogerson. *'The Importance Of Greenspace For Mental Health.'* BJPsych International 14, no. 4 (2017): 79–81, page 51

24 Nieuwenhuis, M. et al. *'The Relative Benefits Of Green Versus Lean Office Space: Three Field Experiments.'* Journal of Experimental Psychology: Applied 20, no. 3 (2014): 199–214, page 51

25 Cooperative Extension Service, University of Kentucky, College of Agriculture. *'Design Expressions: Fact Sheet 4: Responding to Color.'* www2.ca.uky.edu/HES/fcs/, page 51

Caroline Till for *Dezeen* 'Marrs Green revealed by GF Smith as "world's favourite colour"', 2017, page 53

26 Human Spaces Report. *'Human Spaces: The Global Impact Of Biophilic Design In The Workplace.'* (2015), page 54

27 Association of Nature and Forest Therapy. *'The Science.'* www.natureandforesttherapy.org/about/science, page 54

28 Taylor, Richard P. et al. *'Perceptual And Physiological Responses To Jackson Pollock's Fractals.'* Frontiers in Human Neuroscience 5, article number 60 (2011), page 66

29 Zanvyl Krieger Mind-Brain Institute. *'Beauty And The Brain: A Neural Approach to Aesthetics.'* Walters Art Museum, 2010, page 70

30 Bar, Moshe, and Maital Neta. *'Visual Elements Of Subjective Preference Modulate Amygdala Activation.'* Neuropsychologia 45, no. 10 (2007): 2191–2200, page 70

31 Vartanian, Oshin et al. *'Impact Of Contour On Aesthetic Judgments and Approach-Avoidance Decisions In Architecture.'* Proceedings of the National Academy of Sciences of the United States of America 110, supplement 2 (2013): 10446-10453, page 70

The Book of Circles © 2017 by Manuel Lima. Reprinted by kind permission of Princeton Architectural Press, page 72

32 Bassili, John N.. *'Facial Motion In The Perception Of Faces And Of Emotional Expression.'* Journal of Experimental Psychology: Human Perception and Performance 4, no. 3 (1978): 373-379, page 73

33 ibid, page 73

34 Pornstein, Marc H., and Sharon J. Krinsky. *'Perception Of Symmetry In Infancy: The Salience Of Vertical Symmetry And The Perception Of Pattern Wholes.'* Journal of Experiemental Child Psychology 39, no. 1 (1985): 1–19, page 74

35 Wignall, Anne E. et al. *'Flower Symmetry Preferences In Honeybees And Their Crab Spider Predators.'* Ethology 112, no. 5 (2006): 510–518, page 74

36 Sasaki, Yuka et al. *'Symmetry Activates Extrastriate Visual Cortex In Human And Nonhuman Primates.'* Proceedings of the National Academy of Sciences of the United States of America 102 (2005): 3159-3163, page 74

37 Edéll Gustafsson, U., and A. Ek. *'The Relevance Of Sleep, Circadian Rhythm And Lifestyle As Related To A Holistic Theory of Health.'* Scandinavian Journal of Caring Sciences 6, no. 1 (1992): 29-35, page 78

References

38 Dana Lynn, Christopher. *'Hearth and Campfire Influences On Arterial Blood Pressure: Defraying The Costs Of The Social Brain Through Fireside Relaxation.'* Evolutionary Psychology 12, no. 5 (2014), page 81

39 Yadlapalli, Swathi et al. *'Circadian Clock Neurons Constantly Monitor Environmental Temperature To Set Sleep Timing.'*, page 81

40 Nature 555 (2018): 98–102, page 83

41 Persil, 'Dirt Is Good', www.dirtisgood.com, page 87

42 University of Chicago Medical Center. *'New Study Shows People Sleep Even Less Than They Think.'* ScienceDaily, 3 July 2006, page 96

43 University Of Colorado Boulder. *'Children Uniquely Vulnerable To Sleep Disruption From Electronic Screens.'* ScienceDaily, 1 November 2017, page 96

44 Figueiro, Mariana G. et al. *'The Impact Of Daytime Light Exposures On Sleep And Mood In Office Workers.'* Sleep Health 3, no. 3 (2017): 204–215, page 97

45 Stothard, Ellen R. et al. *'Circadian Entrainment To The Natural Light-Dark Cycle Across Seasons And The Weekend.'* Current Biology 27, no. 4 (2017): 508–513, page 97

46 Cajochen, Christian et al. *'Evidence That The Lunar Cycle Influences Human Sleep.'* Current Biology 23, no. 15 (2013): 1485–1488, page 98

47 Wolverton, B. C. et al. *'Interior Landscape Plants For Indoor Air Pollution Abatement.'* NASA Technical Report, 15 September 1989, page 106

48 Zhang, Long et al. *'Greatly Enhanced Removal Of Volatile Organic Carcinogens By A Genetically Modified Houseplant, Pothos Ivy (Epipremnum aureum) Expressing The Mammalian Cytochrome P450 2e1 Gene.'* Environmental Science and Technology 53, no. 1 (2019): 325–331, page 106

49 Indoor Air Quality Scientific Resource Bank. *'Ventilation Rates And Office Work Performance.'* https://iaqscience.lbl.gov/vent-office, page 109

Biophilic Cities, by Timothy Beatley. Copyright © 2011 by the author. Reproduced by permission of Island Press, Washington, D.C., page 109

50 Ward, Adrian F.. *'Winter Wakes Up Your Mind –And Warm Weather Makes It Harder To Think Straight.'* Scientific American, 12 February 2013, page 111

51 Kloc, Joe. *'Putting Insomnia On Ice.' Scientific American, 1 November 2011, page 111*
52 Williams, Lawrence E., and John A. Bargh. 'Experiencing Physical Warmth Promotes Interpersonal Warmth.' Science 322, no. 5901 (2008): 606–607, page 111

53 Bargh, John A., and Idit Shalev. *'The Substitutability Of Physical And Social Warmth In Daily Life.'* Emotion 12, no. 1 (2012): 154–162, page 112
54 Balling, John D., and John H. Falkin. *'Development Of Visual Preference For Natural Environments.'* Environment And Behavior 14, no. 1 (1982): 5–28, page 117

55 Li, Qing. *'Effect Of Forest Bathing Trips On Human Immune Function.'* Environmental Health and Preventative Medicine 15, no. 1 (2010): 9–17, page 119

56 Lee, Kate E. et al. *'40-Second Green Roof Views Sustain Attention: The Role Of Micro-Breaks In Attention Restoration.'* Journal of Environmental Psychology 42 (2015): 182–189, page 122

57 Franklin, Deborah. *'How Hospital Gardens Help Patients Heal.'* Scientific American, 1 March 2012, page 124

58 Shanahan, Danielle F. et al. *'Health Benefits From Nature Experiences Depend On Dose.'* Scientific Reports 6 (2016): 28551, page 127

59 Natural Resources Institute Finland (www.luke.fi/en/), page 127

60 De Bloom, Jessica et al. *'Exposure To Nature Versus*

Picture credits

Relaxation During Lunch Breaks And Recovery From Work: Development And Design Of An Intervention Study To Improve Workers' Health, Well-Being, Work Performance And Creativity.' BMC Public Health 14, article number 488 (2014), page 127
61 White, Mathew et al. *'Blue Space: The Importance Of Water For Preference, Affect, And Restorativeness Ratings Of Natural And Built Scenes.'* Journal of Environmental Psychology 30, no. 4 (2010): 482–493 , page 134

62 Kim, Gwang-Won et al. *'Functional Neuroanatomy Associated With Natural And Urban Scenic Views In The Human Brain: 3.0T Functional MR Imaging.'* Korean Journal of Radiology 11, no. 5 (2010): 507–513, page 137

63 Gould van Praag, Cassandra D. et al. *'Mind-Wandering And Alterations To Default Mode Network Connectivity When Listening To Naturalistic Versus Artificial Sounds.'* Scientific Reports 7, article number 45273 (2017), page 144

The Great Animal Orchestra by Bernie Krause. Reprinted by permission of Profile Books, page 146

64 European Commission Science for Environment Policy. Thematic Issue: Noise Impacts On Health 47 (2015), page 147

65 Shield, Bridget M., and Julie E. Dockrell. *'The Effects Of Noise On Children At School: A Review.'* Building Acoustics 10, no. 2 (2003): 97–116, page 147

With huge thanks to a handful of print sellers who have very kindly allowed us to reproduce their images of original prints.

Thank you to Hermione Stewart at Paper Popinjay Prints who sells beautiful antique prints from 18-20th centuries. In *Biophilia* we have used many images from her collection of illustrations by Anne Pratt, a 19th century English botanical illustrator. www.etsy.com/uk/shop/PaperPopinjay

Thank you to Nina Eichner at Ninska Prints who has a wonderful collection of maps, etchings and lithographs. www.etsy.com/uk/shop/NinskaPrints

Also thanks to Nav Andrade of She Prints Vintage who owns a quirky collection of original prints. www.etsy.com/uk/shop/ShePrintsVintage

Hermione Stewart at Paper Popinjay: cover, pages 4, 5, 15, 16, 17, 18, 19, 36, 37, 38, 39, 45, 63, 77, 133, 143, back cover

Nina Eichner at Ninska Prints: pages 6, 7, 13, 25, 34, 35, 116, 117, 122, 124, 146, 160

Nav Andrade at She Prints Vintage: pages 99, 152, 153, 154, 155, back cover

Shutterstock: pages 67 top right, 72 top left, 93,94, 102 top

Stockfresh: Page 135

P Library of Congress, Prints & Photographs Division, HAER CAL, 54-THRIV.V,2--17: page 29

Woods 69/12147 from The Contemporary Collection, £85 per 10m roll by Cole & Son. www.cole-and-son.com: pages 30-31 and back cover

Mary Evans: page 113

Illustrations by Ernst Haeckel: pages 64, 65, 68, 71, 72

Dover books: pages 10, 14, 47, 61, 67, 74, 75, 102, 107, 123, 126, 127, 128, 129, 147 insect, 149 plant

Creative Market: backgrounds on pages 24, 42, 62, 76, 100, 114, 132, 142

Helen Bratby: pages 20, 26, 27, 68, 71, 72, 80, 82, 84, 85, 86, 89, 104, 105, 110, 121, 130, 131, 138, 139, 140, 141, 145, back cover

Sally Coulthard: pages 2, 23, 40

Index

Acknowledgements

What a fun book to work on. As always, a huge thanks to Jo Copestick for seeing the potential in an unpronounceable subject and being the loveliest publisher to work for.

Isabel Gonzalez-Prendergast - thank you for all your editorial patience, Caroline Alberti for your production par excellence, and the ever delicious Sian Parkhouse for her copyediting.

But most of all, thanks to Helen Bratby. When we sat in a bar thinking over this book and I said I wanted something a 'bit odd', you took that kernel and grew it into the most deliciously mad, beautiful, stylish book an author could wish for. Drinks on me next time.